WAR, ICE & PIRACY

War, Ice & Piracy

The Remarkable Career of a Victorian Sailor

The Journals and Letters of Samuel Gurney Cresswell

Edited by Dominick Harrod

CHATHAM PUBLISHING

LONDON

Dedication
For W H
from her grateful son

First published in Great Britain in 2000 by Chatham Publishing,
61 Frith Street, London W1V 5TA

Chatham Publishing is an imprint of Gerald Duckworth & Co Ltd

British Library Cataloguing in Publication Data
A catalogue record for this book is available from the British Library

ISBN 1 86176 138 4

Typeset by Dorwyn Ltd, Rowlands Castle, Hants
Printed and bound in Great Britain by the Cromwell Press, Trowbridge, Wilts

Contents

List of Plates

Preface

From 1842 to 1862, my great–great–great uncle, Samuel Gurney Cresswell, was a sailor in Queen Victoria's Navy. This book is the story of that naval service. If it should be asked, 'Why another book of naval adventures, battle and endurance?', the answer is that Cresswell's career was extraordinary: in a peacetime Navy, when many officers found it impossible to get any sea-time, he contrived to serve (and fight) in theatres as far apart as China and the Baltic, and is widely understood to be the first man to traverse the North-West Passage.

The case for Cresswell is strengthened by his capacity as an artist, as well as a sailor. For the last fifty years his dramatic lithographs of the Arctic voyage of the *Investigator* have hung on my walls, from rooms at university a good many years ago, to my present Norfolk cottage facing the North Sea, which was so familiar to him.

They provide his credentials as artist. As sailor, his sword and epaulettes, and the scroll presented to him by his fellow citizens of King's Lynn on his return from the North-West Passage, repose in a glass case upstairs in my parental home, and his likeness as a young man gazes down from the wall. He was for me, by family history, and the trophies he left behind, *the* Norfolk hero.

By the same chance, a bulging bundle of his letters home from all over the world descended to my generation of the family. When, a few years ago, I began to sift them, I found a much more complex and revealing archive than the familiar pictures from the icy regions. Cresswell had experienced life in the Victorian Navy from youth to maturity. His life was one of hardship and near-disaster, as well as excitement, adventure and the pleasure of foreign travel and discovery, especially in the Orient.

It was quite a task to decipher the hundreds of letters in their red-ribboned bundles, not opened since his mother had tied them up labelled 'Arctic', 'Baltic', 'China', 120 years ago. The letters breathed in every line the world of the Victorian Navy.

More than this, Cresswell was, from his earliest youth, a painter of great skill. The sketches which illustrate this volume are testimony to an eye, and a talent with pen and brush, uncommon even by the high standards of draughtsmanship essential for navigators in the Navy before the days of the camera.

This book is the result. With the help of other sources, such as Captain Sherard Osborn's *Discovery of the North-West Passage*, and Clowes' *History of the Royal Navy*, it tells the story of one sailor and his friends for twenty years at sea from the 1840s to the 1860s. This book does not aspire to naval scholarship, nor, except as reflected in Cresswell's letters, seek to comment on or re-open old battles or controversies surrounding the conduct of British fleets at sea, and their commanders, good or bad. But it may be worth observing that some of the things he said about the conduct of the British Baltic fleet in 1854 would, had they reached the press, have caused major controversy, and probably ended his career there and then.

But what I do claim for much of this book is its authenticity. With the exceptions mentioned above, the sources are primary. The reader will be reading over my shoulder the letters and journals written by Samuel Gurney Cresswell, his colleagues and his relations at the time of the events recorded. This sometimes sets the existing record straight. At least one account of the M'Clure expedition in the Arctic, says that the store ship *Breadalbane* sank shortly *after* HMS *Phoenix* had set out for England with Cresswell, and Lieutenant Wynniatt, the sick mate of the *Investigator* on board in 1853. In fact, (see pp 92-3) Cresswell witnessed the sinking of the *Breadalbane* from on board the *Phoenix*, which did not set out for home for another three days.

Finally, I do not claim more than a casual knowledge of seamanship, and I hope ocean-going readers will excuse solecisms regarding the setting of sails, or their management which may have slipped through from Cresswell's sailor's handwriting to the printed page. I ask this indulgence for one who, while an occasional sailor, has made a habit of keeping the shore in sight at all times.

MAPS

The three sketch maps are based on charts of the day. Many names used are not to be found in current atlases, but correspond to the names used in the text. 'Banks Land' in the western Arctic is a case in point, since later authorities call it 'Banks Island'. However, Cresswell called it 'Banks Land' in labelling his sketches, as so it was known to the crew who wintered three years on its frozen shores.

A handful of well-known present-day cities are included to assist orientation, but the maps are designed to do no more than locate the areas of Cresswell's activities in the Arctic, Baltic and South China seas. I am very grateful to the artist, Nicholas Hamond, who has faithfully carried out the sometimes awkward task of including what is important to the story with admirable clarity and lack of clutter.

Introduction

The middle years of the nineteenth century saw the transformation of the Royal Navy. At the opening of the period the Navy was recognisably the same as the fleet which secured the victory of Trafalgar under Nelson in 1805. The wooden hulled sailing ships exemplified even today by HMS *Victory* gave the Navy an appearance which in essentials went back centuries. As late as 1842 the 70-gun *Cumberland* sailing man-of-war was launched, only three years after the *Queen* of 110 guns. But even as Sir William Symonds, naval architect of these giant sailing vessels, was introducing improvements which brought his ships close to the limits of sailing power, two great technological changes were already well under way.

These were the arrival of steam for power and iron for hull construction. The vulnerable paddle-wheel restricted the value of steam to frigates and smaller vessels, but the advent of the underwater screw propeller in the late 1840s speeded up the adoption of the new power-source in the Navy's big ships. By the middle of the 1850s whole battlefleets were going into action driven by steam, and smaller ships constructed of iron had also experienced battle. However, the machinery was unreliable and coal-hungry, so mast and sails were retained for economy and cruising range. But in many features these ships were the recognisable forerunners of twentieth century naval vessels.

The change in design and the coming of steam also led to great changes in tactics, and what was required of officers and men, to exploit the new ability to steam to windward, and of course to outmanoeuvre sailing opponents at sea. Facing these momentous changes, the Navy was commanded by an ageing officer class, and presided over by an Admiralty of conservative tradition. Considering these factors, it is surprising how quickly the technological changes swept through the fleets of Queen Victoria, so that in 1856, only a quarter-century after the building of the first naval steam-driven vessel, the grand Spithead review was described by a participant as 'a large manufacturing town under weigh', as the Channel Fleet steamed, rather than sailed, in line.

That the Navy found itself under the command of an ageing and sometimes cautious officer class during these years arose from the rules and conventions governing promotion in the service. These rules provided that promotion after Captain was by simple seniority, and before it by an unpredictable combination of 'interest' (political or social influence) and distinguished service, usually in battle. At the same time, when the demands of the Navy fell dramatically, as at the close of the Napoleonic Wars, large numbers of officers were placed on half-pay with nothing to do, but they did remain on the Navy List.

The size of the peacetime Navy, according to Sir William Laird Clowes in *The Royal Navy** was minute in comparison with the wartime maximum strength. Thus from 99 ships of the line, and 495 cruisers in 1813 at the height of the War of 1812 with America, commissioned strength was cut within four years to 13 ships of the line and 89 cruisers: 594 vessels had shrunk to 102. For the men and officers the effects were drastic. A total of 140,000 seamen and Royal Marines were serving in 1813; but by 1817 that number had been cut to 19,000, a six-fold decrease alongside the five-fold reduction in ships.

In the wardrooms of the Navy the impact was equally drastic, but different in effect. Schemes of compulsory retirement for officers of Captain's rank or higher were limited, and the provision for voluntary retirement by Lieutenants or Commanders (the lower wardroom ranks) was meagre. In consequence the lists became enormously clogged up, especially as many deserving officers were promoted to Captain's rank at the end of the war in 1815. By 1818, there were 883 Captains in the list, the all-time high for the Navy so far. After eventual reforms in 1856, the

---

* *The Royal Navy, A History from the Earliest Times to the Present*, by Sir William Laird Clowes, in seven volumes, first published 1901. This standard work on the Navy is marked by detailed factual accounts laced with Clowes' often blunt opinions on naval matters and policies.

number of Captains was cut to a more realistic 389, but as will be seen, this still left many of them unemployed.

The main difficulty was that flag officers (Admirals) were by rule chosen from the longest-serving Captains. This meant that Admirals had to come from the ranks of Captains who had held that rank at least since Trafalgar. Clowes draws the moral: 'The senior one of them was about 68 years of age; several were over seventy; and one at least was as much as seventy-eight. Yet it was from among these old gentlemen that the list of Admirals had to be recruited.'

This may sound like a dry statistical conjunction, caused by the welcome ending of the wars, and of no great significance in peacetime, but events were to show that the age of officers could have a major impact on naval conduct. In 1854, the Navy fielded a fleet in the Baltic which combined two of the features so far discussed. The fleet included a squadron of steam-driven vessels, the first ever sent in harm's way, marking a great breakthrough for the technology. But these ships were under the command of Admiral Sir Charles Napier, who was at the time sixty-eight years old. Clowes observes: 'During the war with Russia, the Navy, all things considered, disappointed the expectations of the country; and it may well be that its comparative failure to effect brilliant results may be traced in some degree to the excessive age of many of the Flag-officers and Captains, all of whom were, of course the products of the system.'

Inevitably, then, the Navy at sea, and the Admiralty at home could fairly be described as conservative. Such conservatism might be manifest in harsh regimes of discipline, little changed since Nelson's day, although individual commanding officers had much discretion in the severity or otherwise of their shipboard regimes.

Senior officers were also open to the criticism of being unduly timid. Such was the view of others as well as Clowes in commenting on the almost complete lack of action by the British fleet in the Baltic. Samuel Gurney Cresswell, the hero of this work, in his letters from the Baltic, where he commanded HMS *Archer*, is forthright in his criticism of the inactivity of the high command. His opinions were probably shared by many of the fleet's younger officers (who were, of course, not privy to the orders under which the admiral operated), but such criticism of the naval hierarchy as he made in his letters home would, if 'leaked' today to the newspapers or media, certainly result in discipline or expulsion from the service. As things fell out, Cresswell saw much service, twice in Chinese waters, in the Baltic, in the Channel fleet, and in Arctic exploration where he shared in the discovery of the North-West Passage. To serve for twenty years, from Volunteer to Captain, was unusual in a 'peacetime' navy, though his service included warlike actions as well as the excitement of exploration and the tedium of blockade patrols. His sea-time had earned him the right to be critical.

The caution bred of maturity of which Cresswell complains, was shared in the Admiralty, and it extended to spheres wider than just the Baltic campaign. Another example was witnessed by Cresswell on the China station during the second Opium War. In 1858 the taking of the Taku forts at the mouth of the Peiho river was not followed up by an attack on Peking as some officers in the Anglo-French force commanded by Lord Elgin would have liked. If this were cautious, the consequences were mixed. On the plus side, the Treaty of Tientsin of June 1858, secured the objectives of the allies, confirming the earlier Treaty of Nankin and providing for access to Chinese ports, toleration of Christianity, and the posting of a British minister at Peking. Less satisfactory was the fact that within a year forts at the mouth of the Peiho river had been entirely reconstructed, probably with the assistance of Russian engineers, and a second assault in 1859 was made necessary when the Chinese declined to allow emissaries from the allies up the Peiho river to Tienstin. These events add weight to the more belligerent view expressed in 1858, that Lord Elgin's force should have pressed on to Peking when the opportunity offered.

In what follows there is very little which reflects badly on the conduct of naval ships in either peace or war, and a great deal which shows ingenuity, effort and bravery in carrying out the tasks set for the ships and crews. But it cannot be denied that there was occasionally frustration at the lack of decisiveness and aggression from above. This, it should in fairness be said, may reflect the eagerness of the younger officers with whom Cresswell served, and among whom chafing at the irresolution of their seniors was then, and no doubt is still, endemic in the wardrooms and messes of the services.

So, in mid-century the Navy was heavily engaged in patrolling, and occasional hostile actions. While many of the senior men seen long service, there were younger officers also making their way up the ladders of promotion, like Commander, later Captain, Sherard Osborn who, in the intervals of a full naval career, found time to write up, from the despatches and logs of Captain Robert M'Clure, a full account of *The Discovery of the North-West Passage* published in 1856, two years after the completion of this epic voyage of the *Investigator* and her crew including the then Lieutenant Cresswell.

The North-West Passage voyage was the most remarkable of Cresswell's adventures, giving him the distinction of being among the first explorers to confirm that the North-West Passage through the often ice-bound Arctic sea did actually exist. His was the privilege of bringing back an account of the discovery to the Admiralty in London. And the adventure, which occupied five years of his naval career, was typical of another aspect of the naval aspirations of the time. Exploration and survey were then, as now, deemed a worthwhile peacetime employment of naval resources by the Admiralty. For many officers, in the absence of a major maritime war, it was seen as the key to an active posting, with the ultimate prospect of promotion. There was never a shortage of officers volunteering for Arctic duty. The intensity of the interest in such voyages is perhaps best illustrated by the fact that in 1853 Cresswell encountered, including his own trapped *Investigator*, at least seven British naval vessels engaged in exploration, relief or supply in the Arctic region.

As is evident from the foregoing, Samuel Gurney Cresswell had a full and varied career in the Navy. By the standards of the day, he saw a great deal, only falling foul at the end of his career to the scourge of the overcrowding of the senior ranks mentioned earlier. He experienced at first hand almost all of the changes of the early Victorian Navy, from sail to steam, from wood to iron, and from a war-fighting to a policing role. He also benefited from the growing professionalism of the mid-century Royal Navy.

Largely as a result of the Navy's poor performance against the Americans in the War of 1812, at least partially attributed to inferior shooting, a new gunnery school was established at Portsmouth on board HMS *Excellent* in 1830. Initially the Naval

College at Portsmouth had only been attended by new entrants to the service, but in 1836 the College was taken over for the training of serving officers on half-pay (that is, between active postings), in gunnery and other skills. Thus when, in 1848, Cresswell spent some time at *Excellent* on a gunnery course he was experiencing a direct consequence of reforms in naval training brought about by the reverses in the war with America.

He also spent some time at Portsmouth in 1855 to be brought up to date with the latest naval technology. This was a good preparation for his last major posting. In 1857-9 he experienced the latest developments at first hand in command of HMS *Surprise*, a screw dispatch vessel, bound for China. By 1857, in the technological development of the Navy's steam ships, the screw had decisively established its superiority over the earlier paddle steamers which were the Navy's first steam-powered vessels. Cresswell was to experience both their advantages and shortcomings.

In the argument between screw and paddle power, the screw had the decisive tactical benefit that it was not vulnerable to gunfire, unlike the above-water paddle – and its engine could be situated low down, beneath the waterline. Furthermore, it did not take up space on the broadside, where most guns were still mounted; this aspect had prevented the construction of any paddle-driven battleships, the earliest steamers being frigates and smaller craft. There were also more subtle points in favour of the screw: in a rough sea it was unaffected by the heeling of the ship, while a paddle-steamer was likely to lose power from one or other paddles mounted on each side of the vessel as the ship rolled; for a given engine power the screw also delivered greater thrust than the paddles.

In 1845 the technological debate was more or less settled in a contest between HMS *Rattler* and HMS *Alecto* each with steam engines of 200 horsepower. *Rattler* was screw driven, *Alecto* the paddle steamer. On a course of 80 miles in calm seas, *Rattler* won by 23½ minutes; on a 34-mile course in a breeze, with sails set, the screw vessel was 13 minutes up, and on a 60-mile course against a head sea, *Rattler* came in 40 minutes ahead. From a publicity point of view, however, the most telling test was a tug-of-war with the two vessels attached stern-to-stern: with both steaming flat out, and the *Rattler* towing the discomfited *Alecto* backwards at 2½ miles an hour!*

Twelve years later, in 1857, Cresswell set out with a flotilla of steam-assisted ships. The virtue of their screw-delivered steam power was just that – considerable power. During the voyage Cresswell found himself towing two or more of his accompanying ships at once. The drawback was that the engines not infrequently broke down, which of course required the very towing of which those still working were capable. A tactical and cruising advantage was, of course, that steam power took no account of the wind, or lack of it, so that the screw vessel could not only steam to windward but, as Cresswell experienced, make progress in the doldrums, as he had to in order to make a rendezvous in Rio de Janeiro in 1857. However, the early boilers were very inefficient and used coal rapidly, so running out of supplies soon came to be a real threat. On any long voyage orders were given not to use the engines except in an emergency or, sparingly, to make up time.

Captains needed ingenuity and luck when, as occasionally happened, orders to conserve coal coincided with a schedule which would require brisk steaming. A prime example of good fortune was Cresswell's chance encounter with a collier when the *Surprise* found herself low on coal half way across the Atlantic in 1857. The hybrid ships, equipped with sail and engines, were the hallmark of this period of the 'transitional' navy. Essentially, a sail or two could steady the ship and reduce rolling when steaming in a seaway, and at other times, with a fair wind, the engines could be shut down, and coal saved. A refinement of these ships was that, under sail, the screw could be 'raised'; that is, detached from the drive shaft and hoisted into a vertical trunking astern, so as to eliminate drag when under sail. This was done by Victorian naval vessels cruising, just as today's dinghy sailor hoists the outboard motor clear of the water when setting sail. Given the problems of early steam machinery so vividly portrayed in Cresswell's letters, it easy to understand why the apparently conservative technology of masts and sails was retained so long after the introduction of steam.

---

* Clowes, *op cit*

While these technical changes were altering the Victorian Navy by leaps and bounds, some aspects of naval life remained unchanged. Ship management involved not only the technical aspects of sail or steam, navigation and victualling, but also the personal relations of command and companionship. In a career of twenty years at sea, Cresswell experienced everything from the discipline of an apprentice, not allowed to go on shore until he had completed his lessons, to the very different problems of leadership.

In his first personal command, HMS *Sparrowhawk*, in the Channel fleet, he found himself frustrated by the convention of having his meals served to him in his cabin, while through the bulkhead he could hear the chatter and laughter of the wardroom where he would until recently have been joining in the fun. But he did not repine and do nothing about the loneliness of command. In his next command, HMS *Surprise*, bound for China, he broke down the conventional distance by arranging games of whist, alternating between the wardroom and his own cabin, to keep in touch with his brother, though now junior, officers. By such means he tried, within the rules, to make long voyages enjoyable as well as efficient. His approach was doubtless influenced by the generosity, and accessibility of senior officers towards him when he had served as apprentice, and as midshipman; and perhaps in contrast to his treatment as a lieutenant under the formidable Captain Sir Robert M'Clure in the Arctic.

It was important that ships' companies got on, because one feature of the Victorian Navy which distinguishes it most sharply from the present, was the lack of communication. Days, weeks or months would pass between the writing of a letter home, and receiving a reply. For example Cresswell might have considered himself lucky to get a requisition of clothes, as a growing boy, from his parents in England to the South China Seas in less than a year! A box of shirts was one thing, orders from the Admiralty quite another, and the Navy was bound to rely immensely on the discretion of its officers at sea to make all but the most strategic decisions.

I have already recorded the evidence that young officers were often impatient with cautious commanders; but the loss of a ship, always a possibility when at war, and sometimes threatened by storm or sea, was a very serious matter for even senior officers. It is not surprising, therefore, that preserving the ship, whatever the operational trial, was the first priority. Against this background, the naval engagements witnessed by Cresswell in China may have seemed timid in the wardroom, but except by accident in the Arctic ice, no ship closely linked to his experience was lost, though many suffered minor damage.

Another aspect of his experience worth attention was naval contact with foreigners encountered during the long voyages away from home. His adventures at Madeira are light comedy; an English family of acquaintances provoke him into a frenzy of smartening up the ship (HMS *Surprise*) to welcome them aboard. The Inuit (Cresswell's Eskimaux) encountered in Greenland in 1848 seem to have been both welcoming and useful, in that they had firsthand news of the all-important weather conditions, and intimate knowledge of the movements of the pack-ice. The Danish Governor of the settlement at Whale Fish Islands provided light relief by over-indulging in the Navy's shared hospitality, in the form of a bottle of rum.

During two visits to Rio de Janeiro, separated by fifteen years, Cresswell observed dryly the effect of the ending of the slave trade which had taken place in the interim; and there are at least hints in 1857 that the English officers were not unreservedly welcome, even if their money was acceptable. Hong Kong and China were very different as, so far as shore contacts were concerned, these were with British expatriates or colonial servants, on the whole welcoming. Coolies were readily available as bearers for picnics, or other excursions into the countryside, including a memorable river trip at Ning Po in 1858.

The nearest Cresswell came to being threatened by foreign contacts was a close encounter with a Russian officer while ashore on an island off the Gulf of Riga. But while an encounter with the Russian military on shore would have been very dangerous, Cresswell and his fellow officers found a village fete in Latvia entirely enjoyable, and apparently they were welcome visitors. Of course there were also hostile encounters, but these were all deliberate, when the ships' missions were aggressive. Cresswell saw his share of blood and violence ashore during operations on the Chinese coast, and during encounters with pirates in Borneo and China.

Another threat was of a very different order when, during a visit to the Philippines in 1843, HMS *Agincourt* had to beat a hasty retreat to escape the effects of an outbreak of cholera. As he writes: 'the day we sailed, there were three men died of the cholera, so we did not sail too soon.' Sickness was a preoccupation of commanders in hot climates, and cruises away from the confines of Hong Kong, to get fresh sea air were routinely undertaken. Some lessons were learnt the hard way, and the crew of a French frigate suffered from an improvident bathe in the waters of Hong Kong harbour in the heat of July 1844: no less than 120 of the crew went sick in consequence of their dip.

At the other end of the globe, a health precaution which might not have been wholly popular was the rigging of ventilators to duct cold, but fresh, air into the lower decks of HMS *Investigator* in the pack ice in the Arctic, the motive being to drive out the fetid but presumably warmer air of the eighty-strong crew's quarters. The temperature of the 'fresh' air was seldom if ever above freezing. But that precaution, along with other measures, meant that all but a handful of the crew survived the three-year ordeal in the ice. It is remarkable that even though scurvy did attack the crew, the disease only weakened, rather than killed, most of its sufferers.

Food was another of the preoccupations of naval commanders. The taking on of stock (live sheep or cattle) was always to be preferred to living off salted or tinned meat.* Indeed, settlements in such remote corners of the globe as the Magellan Straits traded on selling cattle to passing ships. Preserved meat and biscuit could be, and was, supplemented by what the crews of survey vessels could obtain by shooting game, of which a good deal was taken by the crew of the *Investigator*. And it was an unexpected windfall in the Arctic to find the brief appearance of fields of wild sorrel, hastily gathered by all hands, being the first fresh vegetable available to the crew for more than two years.

Such were the hazards of naval life 140 years ago. They ranged from cholera in the east, to scurvy in the frozen north, from pirates who still today harass the shipping in the South China Sea, to the

---

*Toxins in the tins of meat carried to the Arctic by the expedition of Sir John Franklin have been blamed as contributing to the debilitation of his doomed crew.

military opponents of British interest in China, and in Russia. These risks were the background, sometimes bursting into the foreground, of the naval life. But that life was, of course, special in the essential respect that, for Samuel Gurney Cresswell and his fellow sailors and officers, the fulcrum of career, and day-to-day living, was the moving deck, the bulkhead of wood or iron, the noise of dirty engines, straining rope, flapping sail, or just the howling Arctic wind.

How Victoria's Navy, and her men and officers coped with change, with 'progress', and above all with service, duty and honour is the theme of these pages, drawn directly from one who knew at first hand the rigours of the sea.

ONE

HMS *Agincourt, 1842-1847*

The achievements of Queen Victoria's Navy were prodigious. Her sailors had to cope with much of the change from sailing ships to the newly introduced steam vessels. Her fleets cruised the oceans from the Pacific to the Atlantic, fought the Russian enemy in Crimean and Baltic waters, and did battle with the Chinese half a world away. As well as wars and the fostering of trade and empire, the naval ships vied with European rivals in voyages of discovery, involving feats of stamina, endurance and courage. A sailor in Queen Victoria's Navy might experience all these things, and one such was Samuel Gurney Cresswell, RN.

The son of a banker, Francis Cresswell, and his wife Rachel, the daughter of Elizabeth Fry, the Quaker prison reform pioneer, Samuel was born, at King's Lynn, Norfolk, on 25 September 1827. One of a family of six brothers and one sister, he was for twenty years a sailor, starting his career in the footsteps of his most celebrated Norfolk predecessor, Horatio Nelson, seventy years earlier. Like Nelson, Cresswell joined the Navy young. Both entered the Service through private influence, known in the Navy as 'interest'.

Nelson boarded HMS *Raisonnable* in London at the age of twelve as a trainee Midshipman. He was taken into the Navy from the parsonage at Burnham Thorpe, not far from King's Lynn, by his uncle, Captain of the *Raisonnable*, Maurice Suckling. Cresswell joined HMS *Agincourt* as a volunteer apprentice at the age of fourteen through introduction to Captain Bruce of the *Agincourt* by his cousin, Baker Cresswell Esq, MP for Northumberland North. For both boys, entry into the Navy was fixed by their families.

Each surmounted the same rigours of the seaman's life, absence from home and uncomfortable quarters for many years before the rewards of promotion brought relative comfort, and both knew

The China Coast, the
South China Sea and the
Philippines.

well the vagaries of the sea. Each achieved unique distinction:
Nelson, hero of The Nile, Copenhagen and Trafalgar. Cresswell,
achieving the circumnavigation of the American continent,
passing through the Magellan Strait to the south, then to be first
across the fearsome arctic North-West Passage in a three-year epic
from 1850 to 1853.

Along with actual battles, including the taking of the city of
Canton, and the Peiho Forts in China, Cresswell patrolled the
Baltic ports of northern Russia to deny the Tsar weapons of war
intended for the Crimea, and his duties included fighting pirates in
the South China Sea where, to this day, yachtsmen and traders arm
themselves against piracy. Both men died young, Nelson in battle at
47, Cresswell, at home, exhausted by the rigours of the Navy, at 39.

In 1842, Cresswell's apprenticeship began. Always devoted to boats and sailing, he lived in the family house which overlooked the tidal quays, and the stately merchants' houses and warehouses of King's Lynn. But while devouring books on the sea and ships, he was less assiduous at his studies. In her journal of her son's life, Rachel Cresswell, wrote:

At that time Harrow, where his brothers had been, was rather under a cloud, and we looked to Eton for various reasons... A private tutor, Mr Hawkes agreed to come for a few weeks to try & make him accept the torch of learning . . . he soon found the case hopeless.

So, thoughts of school were abandoned, and the naval career of the next twenty years was launched.

Lynn, Feb 17, 1842

My dearest Papa,

I am delighted to hear that you have got me my appointment. I hope that it will be in one of the ships that are going to China for three reasons.

1st that I most likely should never have the chance of seeing it at any future time

2ndly that I should see a little service and

3rdly I might get a little prize money. I hope you will think me improved in my spelling.* I do not fear much for my writeing. I have not learned the compass yet, but I have such a bad cough that I cannot attend to anything but I shall try to learn it before you come home.

    Your very affect. Son

    S.G.Cresswell

Cresswell's hope was gratified. He was appointed to HMS *Agincourt*, a 74-gun sailing ship of the line built in 1817, the flagship of Admiral Sir Thomas Cochrane, who was going out to

---

* In some of these letters I have retained Cresswell's boyish spellings as vivid evidence of his age. By the end of the four-year voyage there was no need for his parents to correct him.

relieve Admiral Sir William Parker in the China seas where Britain was to sign the Treaty of Nanking later in the year. The Admiral took passage east in a frigate, and *Agincourt*, commanded by Captain Bruce, was ordered to follow the Admiral out. Her course was via Madeira and Rio de Janeiro. In addition to the regular crew, *Agincourt* was shipping 200 sailors to man the Pacific fleet as replacements for men lost or invalided out of other ships.

And among those on board were the 30 volunteer apprentices including Cresswell.

HMS *Agincourt*, Plymouth, April 28th, 1842

My Dearest Mother,

We are now in the sound. We came here this morning and Capt. Bruce and Lady Bruce came on board at 5 O'clock this morning, and then we came here towed by two steamers.

We fired 15 guns when we arrived here. It is about 3 miles from Devonport. We sail on Sunday or Monday next. I have been to the mizzen and main top.

I have a very nice servant. He wants 8s a month, and my mess will cost me 1s 8d a day. We have a very good mess. I begin my log book today and Capt. Bruce makes us keep an account of the money we spend. At 6 O'clock in the morning we turn out, put on clothes and go on deck. At 7 we go down to the cockpit and wash and dress and at 8 have breakfast. At 12 we have dinner and have tea at 6 and we go to bed between 9 and 10. All the lights are put out at 10 except a dim little lamp, so I like to turn in before 10.

April 29th

It is blowing very fresh this morning, but there is very little sea inside the breakwater. The powder came on board yesterday.

May 6th

My dearest Mother

I thought that my last letter was the last from Old England, but the Gods of the winds have decided differently for the very morning we were going to sail the wind changed from fair to foul and it came on very thick.

24

There are 63 sleep in the cockpit, last night my hammock slung in a very nice place for hot weather just under the ladder by which we come down. It is just under the hole that the ladder goes through to the lower gun deck and then to the upper, so that instead of about six inches above my head I have nearly 20 feet.

HMS *Agincourt*, at sea, Monday May 9th, 1842

My dearest Mother and Father,

We sailed yesterday from Portsmouth. We got under way with a nice little breeze, but it was dead against us. Just as we got opposite the breakwater there came on a very heavy squall and we were obliged to reef top sails and lower top gallant sails. We then sailed along finely & sea sickness soon began to appear & by the evening all the volunteers, 30 in number except me, Huthwaite and another chap were sick, you may fancy the agreeableness of the cockpit, a great many are not by any means right yet.

We have got a most beautiful breeze & have just passed a French brig and almost wished it had been war time to have had a bit of a fight.

May 12th

There are most of the fellows quite recovered but there are three miserable sick yet and Russell is one of them. Capt. Bruce is very kind & will often come and talk to one or the other of us. I will now give you a description of a day at sea:

At 4 I had to turn out, for it was my morning watch & then I had to make coffee for the watch. There is a Lieutenant, a Mate, a Midshipman and 4 volunteers in our watch.

Then we all set to work to drink coffee. At half past eight we breakfast, then I read till dinner at one. After that we all gather round the band which plays from about ½ past 3 to ½ past 4 & we fight and throw our caps about while the band plays and after read or draw till tea time. After that we watch till eight & we were allowed to go forward to the forecastle.

We have boxing gloves, foils and single-sticks so we have capital fun fighting. There were almost all the officers there & the commander came & looked on & seemed very much pleased.

May 16th

Yesterday was Sunday & a beautiful day it was. We had no service, I suppose they never have while the ship is sailing, but the Captain had some of us into his cabin & made us read the psalms for the day and lessons. Next Sunday we are all to go into the Admiral's cabin and read the Bible with him, all the volunteers.

The wind came fair on Sunday morning and we have sailed away beautifully ever since. On Saturday we rolled a great deal. There was tremendous confusion in the Gun Room, with desks, books, chairs &c &c tumbling from one end to the other.

The Mates and Midshipmen are allowed to smoke if they keep us from smoking. I feel that a glass of beer would not hurt me, but report says that Captain Bruce is going to manage that we should have something. It would be quite a blessing.

We expect to arrive at Madeira tomorrow.

May 18th

The other day there was a man flogged for being drunk. He had 4 dozen lashes, it was very dreadful to hear them, I could not look. We were all obliged to be on deck. The Capt. was so much affected that he could hardly read the articles of war.

May 19th

We have plum pudding every other day, though it is tremendously heavy and at home I would hardly have touched a bit of it. I now eat it most ravenously. I have been working very hard at my watchbill, as there was a report that we must not go on shore till it was written out. In a watchbill you have to write the name of every person on board the Ship.

The weather is getting very warm. We are now, this morning, about 70 miles from Madeira, so we expect to see the island this evening.

HMS *Agincourt*, Rio de Janeiro, July 4th, 1842
My dearest Father and Mother,

I think my last letter ended the day before we arrived at Madeira. We anchored in the bay at 10 O'clock.

The view from the bay is lovely. The green of the vineyards is beautiful and as the lower part of the island is all covered with vineyards it looks like bright green fields.

The Consul came on board directly we cast anchor and we fired a salute of 19 guns to the Portuguese flag and 9 guns to the British Consul on his boarding the ship. At 11 O'clock Mr Gordon came on board and I gave him my letter to take to Mrs Gordon. The Capt. went on shore with Mr Gordon and was kind enough to take about 20 of us on shore in his gig.

We all hired horses and away we went in a body of about 40 galloping through the town. We went up to the Mount and than came down, and after that there were a party of us went up to the highest point in the island and as tremendous a road up to it you can't fancy without seeing it.

In some places it is not more than three feet and a half broad and one side quite steep, and the other a tremendous precipice, in some places a thousand feet deep, and dreadfully rough.

We went up about three thousand feet. I think about half way up was the most beautiful view, as when we got to the top we were all among the clouds. Nothing could content my messmates than to galop down these tremendous roads. I should have thought it quite impossible without I had seen it myself and gone myself.

It was about six in the afternoon that we saw, spread on a long table a most beautiful dinner which I was not very sorry for as I had not had anything to eat since breakfast except a piece of bread and some Madeira. Nearly every cottage is a wine shop, that is you can buy wine; they hand it out in tumblers, and they only charge about 4 pence for nearly half a pint capital wine. After a glorious dinner which I did good justice to we all went on board and reported ower selves at about 9 O'clock.

The next day we went on shore and met Mr Gordon and his sons and we went to his house in the town and had a capital dinner. We rode up to the ranch which is about 4 miles from the town. There we saw Mrs Gordon and after a little refreshment we went out in the garden and gathered oranges off the trees.

We rode down to town and then went on board. We sailed next morning at ½ past three and we had capital breeze for 6 or 7 days and then a great many calms and got into the Variables until three or four days ago.

We have had a beautiful voyage, and arrived here last Saturday which was the 25th of June. It is now the 1st of July and we expect to sail on the 4th. They will not let us have horses because they say that the English

27

officers use the horses so badly that they will not let them out to hire. Yesterday there were two of ower Mates dressed up in foreign dress, great jack boots, blue striped trousers, white jackets and straw hats and they went into a stables and got horses.

There are a great many slaves here and there is one English frigate, two sloops and two steamers besides a great many merchant ships.

HMS *Agincourt*, August 29th, 1842

My dearest Parents,

I have a great deal to say since leaving Rio. We have had a most beautiful voyage until a few days ago, when from a spanking fair breaze which brought us into sight of Java head, we had some gales of wind rounding the end. One night she rolled tremendously, in one lurch she carried away ower after cock pit ladder, and unfortunately an officer was on it and was thrown over into the cock pit very much to the amusement of us. Three or four chests went adrift, a man got his arm broken so that they were obliged to take it off. That day it was such a tremendous roll that the guns on the Quarter deck touched the water.

September 2nd

We are now anchored at Anyer*. We arrived here the day before yesterday after beating about in sight of land for about five or six days oweing to head winds and calms.

I have had a very bad illness but now am quite recovered. I had a little cough for about a week after sailing from Rio and after we had been about a month at sea, I was laid up in the sick list with a dreadful sore throat. I had the feavour very bad and it was not very comfortable with my hammock down in the cock pit. I had only kept it down two days when the Capt. had my hammock taken up to the Admiral's side cabin with another youngster who was afterwards very dangerously ill.

As soon as I might eat I had the chance, for the Captain asked me to dinner for a week running which quite got up my strength. They bleed me in the first part of my feavour. There were seventy in the list at one time, but we have not lost a single man by illness.

But I am sorry to say that two have been lost in the following way. It was on a Friday that I was overhauling my chest when I was startled by

---

* On the north-western tip of Java, facing Sumatra.

the cry a man overboard. The ship was brought to and the cutter manned and lowered but it was to late. The Monday after I dined with the Capt. and after dinner we as usual had reef topsails, and a man was coming down the mizzen topmast rigging. He slipped and fell. He struck against the mizzen chains. He was killed for they saw him floating for a second or two. He did not move, and then went down. The boat was lowered and every thing done that could be.

I was suprised how little the Capt. seemed to be affected. The very next day as we were just setting down to dinner we saw a man swimming. He was a beautiful swimmer, he had fell from the fore rigging, was picked up. The man with one arm is quite recovered and will be soon sent home.

This is a very curious place, and you can get fowls at a rate of five pence a piece. Bet you have not heard of Anyer before. It is in the straight of Sunda.

HMS *Agincourt*, Hong Kong Bay, Nov 9th, 1842

My dearest Father,

We have had capital fun with cricket lately, we have had two matches with the *Cornwallis*. The first we beat them by 1, the second, 15.

This climate is very sickly. We lost two men today in the hospital ship, and have lost about 30 in the last two months, I think 70 since we have been in here.

Since ower first arrival in China the Hospital ship seems to be quite useless. Out of about 50 we have sent, three have come back cured, 30 died.

We have got ower sails bent and are going round the other side of the island tomorrow for the good of the ship's co[mpany]'s health.

Nov 10th

We are under weigh; we got under weigh at two bells this morning and shall be round by 10 o'clock. It is now 7.

7 pm: We are at anchor in Titan Bay after some capital work (this is Friday, bad luck to it) about 11 AM there came on a smart breaze. We had just tacked, a squall came, split ower Fore topsail, Main Ditto and Main T.Gl sail, and sprung ower Main Topsail yard. We were quite land-locked at the time. Since then we have split the Main Top Gallant Sail and Jib.

I think I get on very well with Navigation. I like it much. Last time we sailed on Friday we got on shore* in Hong Kong Bay.

The Admiral is very strict about youngsters being out of the ship for more than a day so that there is no chance of my going to Canton. He is so particular because he does not like us to miss School. I think it will be different when we pass for Midshipmen in about four months' time.

Nov 11th

I was delighted to hear of Frank's change of prospects. I think the Army is a very fine profession, and I do not see any objection to going out to India.

I think very differently than I did. From my letters from Plymouth you must have thought that I was disgusted with the service and frightened of going abroad. I am now very glad that I came.

Nov 12th

I dined with the Admiral the other day. He was very civil, but he is known to be a smooth tongued old fellow.

We have quite enough to keep us employed now that the Admiral is on board. There are five of us that take the orderly boat by turns. It is a message boat to the Admiral & takes letters on shore. And then we have to take them up to the different houses, perhaps a mile or so up the hill.

March 1st, 1843

My dear parents,

Sir William Parker arrived here about three or four days ago in the *Cornwallis*. The Captain spoke to him about my remaining in this ship and I think that it is finally fixed that I should remain.

Both Admirals are remaining here in expectation of the return despatch from England. This Admiral expects that Sir W Parker will be ordered home. Sir W Parker expects to remain out, and Sir Thomas Cochrane to go home!

I have had a bad cough and I sleep in the Sick Bay and am excused night watches until my cough gets better.

---

* 'got on shore' = ran aground. In the next few months, Cresswell's view of Hong Kong as a station improved, as he made friends on shore and entered into the life of the Colony.

The *Agincourt* has been more than a year in commission and in 13 more days I shall have been a year in HM Service.

March 3rd

There have been five Court Martials on board this ship. One on the Boatswain of the Brig *Pelican* for drunkenness. The other on a Lieut of HM Brig *Wolverine*. He was turned out of the service for the same thing after having served 11 years. A mate, his brother was turned out but a few days before without a court martial for the same thing.

Our Admiral was President and all the court was rigged out in full uniform.

HMS *Agincourt*, Hong Kong, March 25th, 1842

My dearest Mother,

I hear that we are to sail for Manila in a few days. We hear that the ship will have to anchor 4 miles from the shore, and from the shore to the town is 3 miles. After Manila we are going to Chusan, and to spend the time cruzing about until about September when we expect to return here, Sir W Parker to be ordered home, and us to be left and Commander in Chief.

Sir W Parker is a very stingy old fellow. The other day he told the agent Navy provisioner that he will skin a flint to save Her Majesty a shilling. I must now go and keep the first watch. I hear that we shall sail on the 28th.

HMS *Agincourt*, Hong Kong, May 24th, 1843

My dearest Mother,

We have been to Manila since I wrote last. We sailed from this place on the 8th of last month, arrived there on the 17th.

The day we arrived I sent my letter on shore to Mr Butler, the next day received a note to ask me to go on shore to stay with him. I asked the Commander, he sayed that he had no objection but I must ask the Captain. The Captain had no objection but I must ask the Admiral, but he must know who the letter was from, who it was that I wanted to stay with. When he had satisfied himself as to all these points he had no objection.

I went and had a capital time of it. At 8 am Breakfast, 9 10 walk to the inn where I was shure to meet some of my mess mates. 12 return to Mr

Butler's and take a siesta. 4 dinner ½ past 5 take a drive or ride. 6 go to a ball or walk to the palace square to hear the bands play. Thus I spent 5 days.

While I was on shore at Manila the cholera broke out and at the same time on board. We sailed on the 27th and notwithstanding our quick departure we lost 10 men by cholera, 1 drowned bathing, 1 falling from the Main top shifting topsail yards, 1 brain fever, 13 in about 10 days. We did not make a straight passage from Manila but spent the time working about at sea. We did not arrive here untill the 20th of this month. I am very glad to say the cholera is quite gone and we have not lost a man for several days.

HMS *Agincourt*, Hong Kong, May 29th, 1843

My dearest Father,

I will begin with a description of our cruise to Manilla. We sailed on the 8th of April, and worked out of the bay, an American frigate in company. That night it fell calm and we came to an anchor. The next morning the frigate weighed, and made for Macao. After church, it being Sunday, we weighed and made all plain sail on a wind, as we say in the Log book. We passed a wreck on a reef of rocks about 6 miles from the Island of Luzon. We arrived at Manila on the 17th, anchored in the 5 fathom water about 3 miles from the shore and 4½ from the town.

I went on shore the next day on the 3 o'clock boat, and went to the cemetery. You must imagine a wall about 10 feet thick surrounding a garden about an acre in size. In the middle is a very pretty little chapel.

They bury their dead not in the garden, but in the wall–places large enough to admit a body. The wall being about 10 foot thick and 14 ft high. After the body is put in the mouth of the hole, there is no inscription but they are numbered. I believe it will hold 2,000 dead. There is a walk on the top, and I walked round. After this place is full, the bodies that were first put in are taken out, and as it takes about 20 years to fill the cemetery the bodies taken out are not much more than bones. These bones are then put into a narrow court bricked up except over head.

After that we drove to the Calzada, a drive open to the sea. The drive is about ½ a mile long where ever body turns out to drive up and down in the cool of the evening for about an hour. After that we went on board in the 9 o'clock cutter.

The day we arrived the Governor sent the consul on board and the Admiral fixed to pay the Governor a visit at a stated time the next day. I suppose you have heard that the Admiral is very fond of state, so the next day the Admiral went in grand state. He landed, there was no guard or any body to receive him. He was in a great way about it, and went off to the ship without seeing him. He wrote a letter for an explanation saying that he was not received as a British Admiral might have been.

The Governor sent an apology and the next visit the Admiral was received as a British Admiral should be.

Just as we left Manila there were going to be no end of balls &c. &c.; but the cholera forced us to cut and run leaving two mates and midshipman and Flag Lieut. Egerton. They were on an expedition to the lakes about 60 miles inland. The day we sailed there were 3 men died of cholera so that we did not sail too soon. The next morning we anchored not far from the shore about 40 miles from Manila, and sent boats on shore to water, but there was no good watering place.

They next day we hoisted the boats in and worked up to Manila. They had returned from the lakes and we met them in a Gun boat about 5 miles from the shore, squared yards and ran out to sea. We sighted the Island of Formosa. The sickness is quite gone out of the ship.

HMS Agincourt, Sept 7th, 1843

My dearest Mother,

I have but time to write a short letter as there is a great deal of work. School all the forenoon, Gun drill all the afternoon, Watch to keep, Hammocks up and down, 2 water divisions, Excersing hands, Clothes lists of your division, Log book, Watch station and Quarter bill division List, Learning Gunnery for the next day &c. &c. &c.

Sir W Parker will go to India the end of this month.

It has been tremendously hot, the thermometer between 90 and 100 in the shade; it's now 89 and this is quite a cool day. Very few of us sleep in the cock pit, we sleep on mats on the main or upper deck. There is no more time as I shall get my leave stopped if I do not write out a lot of Gunnery.

HMS *Agincourt*, Hong Kong Bay, Sept 19th, 1843

My dearest Parents

I write home for some clothes &c. I hope you will send them out by the first chance. I believe that there are ships sail from Portsmouth to China every month. The things I wish for are 3 dozen cotton socks, 2 dozen fine duck Trowsers, 2 dozen shirts, enough fine blue cloth to make two jackets and 1 pair of trousers. Naval jacket buttons for 3 jackets, 2 dozen white Pocket Handkerchiefs. My foot is nine inches long now and the trowsers and shirts for a person rather under 5 feet they will be the propoer size for me. I think if you put them in as small a box as you can, if it was lined with tin it would be all the better. I shall expect them out in 6 or 7 months time.*

I am very happy, and a very dull time it is, the only fun we have is bathing, and as you may fancy we swim very well. We have been a long time cruising, so that I do not forget my seamanship. If I shall be anything, I shall be a good seaman.

P.S. 1 dozen Towels and three or four pillowslips will be acceptable.

HMS *Agincourt*, at sea, October, 1843

My dearest Mother,

We are now on a cruise to sea for the benefit of the ship's Co. as Hong Kong is rather sickly and we had 80 in the list. We had been 9 days at sea yesterday and went into Hong Kong to ask if we might go to sea for a few days more. The cutter went on board the flag ship with the Admiral, and he asked we did not anchor but cruise about the Bay, but unfortunately we got on shore and had a great bother getting off.

I quite forgot to give you a description of the Mandarins that have been at Hong Kong. One was the uncle of the Emperor. They came to settle some thing about the treaty†. It was a grand occasion and I went

---

* The clothes arrived nine months later, in June.
† The Treaty of Nanking was concluded and signed on 29 August 1842 on board HMS *Cornwallis* between Sir Henry Pottinger, Britain's Chief representative, and the Chinese plenipotentiaries. Admiral Sir William Parker and Major-General Sir Hugh Gough were the Naval and Army commanders of the successful forces. No doubt the delegation of Mandarins to Hong Kong a year later witnessed by Cresswell concerned execution of the terms which included an indemnity of $21m and the establishment of the treaty ports in China.

to see it. The Chinese went in grand procession from the house where they were staying to that of Sir Hy. Pottinger: and a very curious procession it was. The Mandarins went in palanquins, 30 or 40 men with silk flags, their executioners, and servants, two or three men blowing trumpets and some other musicians were the chief part of the procession.

I had a capital sight of them.

HMS *Agincourt*, Victoria Bay, Hong Kong, Jan 3rd, 1844

My dearest Mother

I hope to write you a long letter this time. We have been a cruise to sea with Sir Wm Parker to try rate of sailing.* The first day the wind was on the quarter. We have all plain sail & Top Gallant Studding sails. I think if anything we rather lost ground on her. The next day we decidedly licked her. We then bore up for Hong Kong and the *Cornwallis* continued to Manila. From thence she is going to Singapore.

Jan 24th

Lately we have been making a survey of the Bay of Hong Kong, and I ought now to be at work at my chart. There is a report that we are going to India in a few weeks. We are painting ship now.

The other day we gave a splendid champagne picnic to the Ward Room officers. It cost us about a pound each and I think about 33 subscribed. It was a very amusing picnic and I will send you a long account when I have time.

HMS *Agincourt*, Victoria Bay, Hong Kong, June 25th, 1844

My very dearest Father,

I have had a delightful trip to Canton, all through the kindness of Capt. Weare. I am delighted with my box, everything fits me to a T.

We sailed for Canton on a Tuesday at 12 o'clock, kept under weigh all night, and were there next day at 9 A.M. I got up at 4 o'clock and saw all there was to be seen from a little above the bar forts. We then got into

---

* The *Agincourt* versus the *Cornwallis*

a little Chinese boat and arrived at Canton at 4 o'clock P.M. The tide was strong against us all the way, but it gave me a capital chance of seeing the boats &c &c on the river. The most funny thing on the river is the Chinese attempt to build an imitation English frigate, but she is very good for the first throw.

The pirates have been at work again. The other day a son of one of the Captains was going from here to Macao, he was attaked and robbed of a gold watch. He put in and reported it. We sent most of ower boats, manned and armed. There was a force of 200 out after them but it was no good. We captured two unfortunate fishing boats, they have been let go.

The night before last about 9 o'clock we heard several guns fired at the bottom of the harbour. We sent a boat but did not find anything except a large merchant's Junk at anchor. She was taken prisoner and kept at anchor near the ship during the night, let go in the morning; a day or two ago a mate of a merchant ship about 9 at night, the boatmen attacked him, cut his throat and shoved him overboard. The boat was chased, but before they came up to her the Chinamen threw the money overboard. The boat was captured and I hope they will be hanged. So much for pirates.

We sail for Chusan on the 1st of September.

HMS *Agincourt*, Victoria Bay, Hong Kong, July 31st, 1844
My dearest Mother,

I am afraid that the ship will remain 2 years more out here. They cannot give the Admiral less than 2 years as commander and chief. The general thing is 3 years as chief in command, but as the Admiral has had 2 years as No 2, they will let him have 2 years in command. It has been dreadfully hot lately, we must be very thankful to have so little sickness on board the English ships.

Five days ago a French frigate here had 4 men in the list. They piped hands to bathe about 2 pm in the hot sea after dinner and today there are 124 in the list.

We have just sent 18 marines on board a merchant's Lorcha that is to take $180,000 to Macao and a Lieutenant. They have got very good information that they are to be attacked by pirates. It is a capital chance for the Lieut. that is going. I wish that they'd let me go.

HMS *Agincourt*, China seas Lat30.45'.0'N Long 123.30'E, September
26th, 1844

My dearest Father,

I am in the sick list with a slight cough and cold. It is the first time I
have been in the list for a year and a half. We left Hong Kong on the 28th
of last month, with the Governor, Mr Davis, HM Sloop *Wolf* in Company.

The monsoon just changing as we left Hong Kong, we stood right
off. It then came on to blow very hard and blew for 4 days. One day it
blew so very hard that we shortened sail to close reefed main topsail; and
fore staysail. It was my morning watch the morning that it blew hardest.
It was tremendous.

I was blown right over to windward merely by the eddy wind from
the main trysail, and the large *Agincourt* had not a dry hand on her deck.
The poor little *Wolf* was seen in the middle watch between
the squalls pretty well smothered as you may fancy. At 5 o'clock it came
on clear and the wind blew less. We could not see the little *Wolf*, and as
she did not outsail us in heavy weather we had great misgivings about her

We then had calms and light fair winds until the 9th when we made
the coast about 90 miles south of Chusan, and the north monsoon set
in then in good earnest but we did pretty well and arrived at Chusan
on the 14th of this month. On our passage we carried away our fore
topsail yard and were three hours shipping it which the Admiral called
very slow and promised to send us out on a cruise of exercise.

The day we arrived at Chusan we had notices that all the impressed
of 5th class had to pass an examination on board the *Castor*; on the 17th
we all passed except one, a very easy exam: only to find how many
dollars is £10 15s, and a question in trigonometry: two sides and an
opposite angle (oblique) to find other side . . . all I did right.

The next day I went on shore to see some of the life of Chusan.

It is a much better place than Hong Kong, and the country is
beautifully cultivated. The Chinese cultivate every inch of ground which
you cannot guess from seeing the barren hills about Hong Kong. The
boats are quite different from the Hong Kong boats. At Chusan there
are 4 and 5 masted junks.

We go in after ower 6-weeks punishment. We are exercised 3 hours
every forenoon and 2 hours every evening. The day before yesterday we
shipped topmasts fore and mizzen. It is dreadful work at sea.

Today we shipped fore topsail yard and mizzen ditto, fore in 20 minutes,
mizzen in 15, very smart . . . The first and middle watches are also

exercised shifting a top gallant mast, a topsail and jib or something, in short with the excercise day and night, quarters of gun drill, logs and working all the things that are required we have not a minute to ourselves. So you may thank my being in the sick list for this long letter. . . . The Admiral has given orders for every day's excersise while we are at sea.

Sept 26th

We now are standing in for Chusan but are not going in. I am much better and I am seventeen today. We are about 8hrs 15mins fast of Greenwich. I intended to wake up this morning to think that it was just at that time you were drinking my health round the dining room table, but I was too sleepy. I have only a slight cough left but they will not let me out of the list. Today we shifted the main topsail yard and jib boom. In sending up the main topsail yard we sprung it in several places. It was made of very bad wood that we made on shore after we sprung one last year.

After we have been out exercising a month, we are to go into Potan to water as there is no good water at Chusan. It is an island of priests and Josses. It will be a fine chance of seeing it.

Nov 13th

We arrived in the outer harbour about 3 weeks ago and the next day the Admiral came out. We sent the barge in for him.

I give you an account of our being inspected by His Excellency Rear Admiral Sir Thomas Cochrane Kt (CB). He came on board the morning after we arrived in the outer harbour. The first thing was to put the boat's mate under arrest for not having boots and straps on them.

We mustered by open list, officers and all. The Admiral made some remarks about some of the midshipmen not having boots on (I had shoes on). Then we mustered by divisions and the Admiral went round all the decks. Two poor unfortunate midshipmen were directed to volunteer again for not having their logs up to date.

HMS *Agincourt*, off Singapore, July 19th, 1845

My Dearest Father

We sailed from Hong Kong on the 3rd of March, and after a very fair passage, arrived at Singapore the 27th. I only was on shore once with my cousin Tom Miller. We had a capital day of it, the nutmeg plantations are very fine. The Admiral did not like the place much and got into a row with the Governor of course, as he has at every place. So we sailed on the 3rd of April and arrived at Penang on the 10th.

I was on shore at the Admiral's house, with my green gig's crew when Russell came in with a list in his hand of young gentlemen to go to India in the *Wolverine*. His and my names were in the list. I was delighted, you know how fond I am of change.

We sailed on the 19th and arrived at Tricomalee 8th May in the most beautiful island of Ceylon. Merchant ships very seldom touch there, it is quite out of the way. I spent a very jolly 5 days on leave, very gay.

During the time I was on the *Wolverine* I kept several watches as officer of the watch, and had to put the ship about, set and take in studding sails, and all sorts of things so I improved my seamanship very much.

Penang is a very nice place, and capital rides about the island. The other day I went in the *Nemesis*, steamer, up a river with the Admiral and had fun and a good ride on elephants. There are a great number of monkeys about the jungle.

July 21st

We are now at anchor about 15 miles from Singapore and expect to sail for Sarawak tomorrow.

Agincourt's mission to Sarawak brought the squadron's patrolling role to an end, with the task of dealing with pirates plaguing the waters round North Borneo and threatening not only the safety of local traders, but as will be seen, the purposes of the East India Company as traders on behalf of British interests. Cresswell's long first cruise in the *Agincourt*, and initiation into the Navy, came to a climax in two short and sharp engagements with the pirates, and introduced him to one of the great characters of the region, Sir James Brooke*, scourge of pirates and Sultans alike.

HMS *Agincourt*, Hong Kong, Sept 30th, 1845

My dearest Mother

We sailed from Singapore on the 25th July and arrived off the river Sarawak the 27th. I forgot to mention Mr Brooke came out to Borneo

---

* Sir James Brooke, Administrator, Hon. East India Company.

and settled about 20 miles up the Sarawak on the S.W. coast of Borneo amongst a set of wild Malays, mostly pirates.

He has succeeded in civilizing the people for some miles around his house. Rajah they call him (that is a sort of Chief). A Captain Bethune came on board at the same time with Mr Brooke. He is sent out to Borneo to make some arrangements about trade with Borneo, and you shall hear why these two gentlemen came on board.

On the 30th we sailed for Borneo Proper, and arrived there on the next day. The pinnace proceeded up the Brunei river with Mr Brooke to pay his respects to the Sultan of Brunei*. The reason of ower expedition was this. The English Government wish to establish trade with Borneo and they are not able to do so because the *pirates* will not allow it.

About three months ago Sir Edward Belcher, was at Borneo Proper. The Sultan then wished to come to some understanding about trade with England and fixed that he should make a treaty in a few months. Soon after this friendly declaration to us he received notice from a Mr Serriff Osman.

His father was a reputable Arab merchant and traded in gold dust with Borneo, who married a Malay woman and this Serriff was the son. His father wished him to follow the old trade, and he did until his father's death and then turned to the most gentlemanly trade of pirating. This naughty son prospered in this more than he did in gold dust trading and became a great chief as you will see.

He was so powerful that he sent this message to the Sultan: if you make any treaty with the English or trade with them in any way I shall come down and burn your town and take you prisoner. The Sultan was in a great fright and communicated to us his fears, and that there were a set of pirates and a pirate chief that would also go against his party if the Seriff invaded the town of Brunei.

Four days after the arrival of us and the other ships, the *Vixen* steamer got her steam up, all ower boats were manned and armed and up we went to the town of Brunei. We arrived there about 3 in the afternoon and then the Admiral and officers were introduced to the Sultan. The Admiral had a long chat with him.

The next day we received a most polite message from the pirate chief to say that if we were not out of the harbour that night he would sink

---

* Omar Ali Suffudee, Sultan of Brunei.

us at our anchors. The Admiral gave him to understand that if he was not out of his house by the next day he would get a dose that he would not like. He was kind enough to let us live that night. The next morning we received a message to ask us why we did not begin. This the Admiral could not stand, and we went down to his house which was truly well fortified, and anchored.

The Admiral did not like to begin the fight. They did not fire. The Admiral then sent a shot just to take the top of his house off. Then they began to fire.

The Admiral then began to fire away, and made the signal to engage. The house was soon dreadfully shattered, and we knocked off firing and landed with the marines. The place was quite deserted and no dead to be found so we left the place to be plundered by the Sultan and his party. The next day we went to the ships and sailed the next.

Arrived at Malloodoo Bay on the 17th August, had a smash fight with Serriff Osman and lost 7 men, and a Mr Gibbard, Mate of the *Wolverine*.

You shall have a good account of Malloodoo Bay in my next letter.

HMS *Agincourt*, Hong Kong Bay, October 20th, 1845
My dearest mother,

I now will give you the best description of ower little action on the north coast of Borneo. I think in my last letter I left the ships off the bay of Maloodoo off the very north of Borneo; the *Agincourt*, *Vestal* 26, *Deadalus* 20, *Wolverine* 16, *Cruiser* 16; *Vixen* Steamer 6, HC* Steamers *Pluto* and *Nemesis*.

The next day all the marines of all the ships were sent on board the *Vixen*, 150 seamen from the *Agincourt* and the same proportion to them from the other ships, about a force of 450. All the boats in the ship armed, I was in the first gig. About 7 am the steamers weighed, and the two brigs, *Wolverine* and *Cruiser*, and I was sent on board the *Cruiser* in my boat, and she being a gig was hoisted on board her. The *Vixen* then took the brigs and away we went up the bay.

It was now about 4 p.m. The boats were now anchored off the *Vixen* in two lines, Capt Lyster commanding the starbord division, Capt Talbot the port. The signal was made to weigh, all the anchors were up, and the

---

* HC = Honourable Company; the ships belonged to the Honourable East India Company's marine.

word was given to give way. We then gave three good cheers and away we went. Just before we got to the mouth of the river, it shoaled to 3 feet so there was no water for our launch, and it was late. The captains thought it was better to anchor for the night until the tide was high enough to pass the bar.

At 11 pm the word was passed to weigh, the tide was high and we crossed the bar and anchored. Every body was just going to sleep when we heard a heavy gun fired not in the direction of the ships. From the report it must be heavy metal and tom tom – tom tom – tom tom &c &c. The order was then passed to load with grape in the gun boats, and load the small arms.

Just as I was going to sleep again there was a small boat seen, and all the gigs and cutters gave chase but he was too fast for us. No doubt he came down to reconnoitre our force. So we went back and I was soon asleep.

At half past four Capt. Lyster roused me up and went alongside Capt. Talbot's boat. I got some breakfast and a glass of wine and water from Capt. Clifford of the *Wolverine*. The word was then passed for all the boats to get their breakfast, after breakfast to weigh, and away we went up the river.

There is thick jungle on each side. It was very beautiful to see 25 boats, most of them very large, mounting guns, pulling up the river all crowded with armed men and marines, all happy, all merry, cheering and talking. The morning was beautifully fine, the scenery was lovely, and the whole gay scene was more like a large party going to a picnic than a battle.

We had got about 5 miles up when all the Captains but one were asked to reconnoitre. We turned a sharp corner of the river and saw a man dressed in white on a 3-gun battery. He seemed to be a very large, fine man, and had a beautiful sword in his hand, waving it to us.

So we returned to the rest of the boats and spread the report that there was one battery with three heavy guns. We then proceeded with the rest of the boats and anchored. Just after we got round the turn of the river to get a little in battle array, down from the battery came a boat with a flag of truce. The person that came in the boat said that Serriff Osman did not wish to fight and wanted to know why we had come up.

We gave the reason and said if he did not clear away the boom that was between us and him in ½ an hour, we would fire on him. He then went back, we weighed and anchored our gun boats by the stern close to the boom. There was so little room that only 10 gun boats were anchored abreast. The rest of the boats anchored by the stern astern of the front row. (The tide was running up all the time). The ½ hour was nearly up when down came the flag of truce again. We now began to work at clearing away the boom.

This time Serriff Osman wanted the leaders of our party to go up. (We afterwards heard from a prisoner that he intended to murder them if he could have got them up). The boat returned. No sooner had she got back than bang went the first gun from the 3-gun battery. That was the signal (the shot had fallen amongst our boats), blaze away was the order given, bang bang bang went the guns on our side rattle rattle went the musketry. In a moment all was noise, smoke and confusion, 11 heavy guns on their side, 10 on board our boats and 3 or 400 muskets blazing away as fast as possible. It is a glorious thing to be in a good hot fight.

Now I must explain why we were kept so long below the boom. It was made of immense trees spiked together by ship's cable and secured round immense trees on shore each side of the river.

Fifty-eight minutes had passed keeping up this most dreadful fire. Many of our men were killed, many wounded. The boats' guns had almost expended all their ammunition, mostly having fired between 30 and 40 rounds, and not a point had been to my eyes gained. But the fine fellows at work on the boom, with our Captain at their head had not been asleep (they had the hottest fire on them all the time). Just as we had been an hour firing, they cleared away a small space.

It was the work of moments for the small boats to get through, and the marines to cross the boom, and get in on the other side. The order then was, give way and take the place at the point of the bayonet.

Directly they saw we had passed the boom, the enemy ran. By this time the boats were all passed and some of the marines landed, and shooting the poor fellows at a dreadful rate. They were jumping out of a further 8-gun battery (invisible until we had passed the boom) and the marines picking them off as they were in the air. There were very few hand to hand fights.

I, with Captain Lyster landed with the first of our party. It was a dreadful sight, men laying about in every direction, some with their heads off, and the most with dreadful wounds. By 10 minutes after the place was taken, all our enemy had fled to the jungle and we were left undisputed masters.

I could tell you dreadful yarns about the sights I have seen but it will only disgust you. We then plundered and burned all the houses, about 30 or 40 in number and returned to the boats, our objective being to get back to the ships before the tide was so low that we could not cross the bar as we had a great many wounded.

In one of our boats one shot killed a man, the next two, and another shot a man's arm away. In the launch we had a man killed, in the pinnace one lost his arm. There were 6 killed on the spot, 18 wounded. Poor Mr Gibbard (mate) of the *Wolverine* was shot through the back, he lived 24 hours afterwards. He was such a nice fellow, I was messmate with him for a month. Another marine died so we lost 8 men. A second mate of the *Vestal* was shot through the leg but is now all right.

We then returned to the ships and were greeted with three hearty cheers. I went down into the *Vixen*'s cockpit, had a good wash, put on clean things, and then had a good dinner. Went to sleep and slept for 13 hours without stopping.

The next day a party were sent to completely destroy the place, and I returned to the ship. We sailed in a few days. Mr Brooke and Capt. Bethune left us and went to Singapore in the brig *Cruiser*. Touched at Manila and arrived here on the 16th September.

For his part in the engagement at Malloodoo, Cresswell was Mentioned in Despatches, a circumstance which he treated, in his next letters home, with a modesty which scarcely veiled his pleasure.

HMS *Agincourt*, Hong Kong, February 27th, 1846

My dearest Parents

I am glad to hear that you liked my letter that I wrote from Hong Kong after the Maloodoo affair. I think that I wrote quite enough about it to last until I come home . . . As to my name in the Gazette it, I am afraid, is not much . . . I think with you, dearest Papa that my appointment to the *Agincourt* was a capital thing.

Capt. Hope Johnston joined the ship the day before yesterday. Yesterday after Church the hands were lined up and Capt Johnston read his appointment to the *Agincourt*. He seems to be a regular service man. I like his look much, he seems to be quite a Gentleman.

I was rather amused and I must say annoyed that that stupid man Shaw put that humbug about me in the Lynn paper. I shall expect a Triumphal Arch to be rigged when I make my entry into Lynn.

I am in the first society in Hong Kong. On Monday I dine with the Chief Justice.

How dreadfully grand Papa must be as Mayor . . .

Dear Papa writes in such a delightful, cheerful happy tone that it has made me as merry as a lark. The ship is very comfortable and every thing in the way that they ought. The Admiral and myself go very well, I must say that I like the Old Gentleman.

It is my middle watch and it has just struck two bells. I shall turn in.

We sail for Calcutta I believe in a day or two. How delightful. I am afraid that it will be rather odd if I deliver my letters (of introduction) more than 4 years old. I shall write from Calcutta if we go.

Cresswell did pay a brief visit to India in the spring of 1846, and managed a couple of weeks' leave on shore during the trip. The *Agincourt* then returned to her home port at Hong Kong.

Her next engagament was once again in Brunei. After the successful foray against Serriff Osman's pirates in 1845, it became apparent that Sultan Suffudee had assumed the role of piracy, and, as William Clowes puts it in his magisterial history of the Royal Navy, committed frightful atrocities against allies of the British. This determined Admiral Cochrane to 'ascend the river to Brunei, and to deal with the Sultan'.

HMS *Agincourt*, Hong Kong, August 14th, 1846

My dearest Father

We arrived here from Malloodoo Bay yesterday, now I must give you some account of our fighting.

After going to Sarawak to get Mr Brooke, we sailed for Brunei and anchored off the river about 8 miles from the mouth.

The first day when some large trading Proas with flags of truce flying were boarded by the Honble E.I. Comp. Steamer *Phlegethon* which boarded one and they gave the information that the Sultan had built some forts up the river, according to the Malays account impossible to pass, but these we could not attack. The next day we weighed and went close into the mouth of the river. The Admiral went up the river. Having seen one fort that was deserted, they sent a boat on shore and spiked the guns and returned to the *Agincourt*.

The next morning I went on board the *Spiteful* with the Admiral, but as there was no room for the green gig to be hoisted up, he sent me on board the *Phlegethon*, and the two steamers proceeded up the river. We anchored off the first fort and sent the *Phlegethon* to bring up all the force.

The next morning the *Phlegethon* came close to at about ½ past 6 o'clock a.m. All the marines embarked on board the *Spiteful* and small arms men; the rocket field piece and mortar parties remained on board the *Phlegethon*. We then weighed and proceeded up the river.

After we had proceeded about 4 miles further up the river we saw ahead two forts, one right ahead and another on a small island near the right bank of the river. The green gig was then lowered down to go ahead of the *Spiteful* to sound.

It was capital fun as we could see the fellows in the fort loading the guns. When we were about 200 yards off they opened fire. The first 3 or 4 shots they fired at the *Phlegethon* as she was the leading steamer, on account of being the smallest and the river not being deep.

After the first 2 or 3 shots they directed their fire towards the *Spiteful,* mostly grape and as the green gig was just on a line between the fort and the *Spiteful* the shot fell about us pretty thick. By this time the *Phlegethon* had ranged close up to the fort and was blazing away. The gun boats had cast off from her and were also firing away and pulling on shore. The rascals then ran. The boats landed but they were all over the hill before our men could get up to the forts. We spiked the guns but left the forts standing as the Admiral was in a great hurry to get up the river on account of the tide. We then moved on again up the river. Just as he opened the town about two miles from the first forts (I forgot to say that after we had passed the forts about a mile, we observed the enemy returning to them. We gave them two or three shots from our long 42-lb guns, and soon saw them running) we opened the town on the Sultan's fort of ten long guns. Immediately we rounded the point they opened fire almost entirely directed against the *Phlegethon*. Immediately she got close to, and the *Spiteful* close astern, and as there was a chance of fighting hand to hand the cowards ran. Some of our people landed and ran after them but an Englishman is no match for a Malay. The Marines were landed and encamped on the hill over the Sultan's house. The town was entirley deserted.

The vile old Sultan had cut into the country. We did not burn the town as 2/3rds of the inhabitants are a harmless set of people.

The next morning the small arms men returned to the ships in the small boats and all the marines except 30 for a guard came on board the *Spiteful* as the weather was very wet and it was uncomfortbale for 350 to be on shore in only 8 small tents. The Admiral, Mr Brooke, Green gig and Staff also remained up the river in the *Spiteful*.

Now the great thing was to nab the Sultan, so they gave the men two days to rest, and the next morning after having breakfast with the Admiral we went on board the *Phlegethon* and all the marines and went up the river ten miles. They disembarked the marines and sent them in the gun boats and the green gig with myself and Admiral, kept company with them until they came to a small creek where the boats turned up. We then parted company.

I went up a high hill with the Admiral where we had a beautiful view of the country for several miles. It was nearly flat, clear from jungle, even in some places nicely cultivated.

We then returned to the *Phlegethon* and steamed down to the town and *Spiteful*, leaving the Sultan hunters to get on the best way they could. I dined with the Admiral that night.

The next day being Sunday they gave the men to rest. On Monday another expedition was sent after the Sultan, but not more successful than the former.

I remained 14 days on board the *Spiteful* with the Admiral up the Brunei river.

One day whilst up the river information came on board the *Spiteful* that Hadji Samon, the Sultan's head man, a most dreadful rascal (in fact it was he that set the Sultan up to all his mischief) was concealed in a village about 20 miles from the town of Brunei. Our force was away after the Sultan at the time and all the men we could muster was a cutter and gig, 20 men in all and our friend Ismail, the brother of Poo Bedradin that was murdered, 18 large Proas and I think about 300 Malays. The Admiral sent me in charge of the gig. We had a very hard day's work but found the houses he had been concealed in deserted, so we burned them. The Malays behaved most admirably, and I had the young Prince in my boat. We were 18 days at and off Brunei and then set sail northward. We routed out several piratical villages towards the north of Borneo and then went to Malloodoo. I went up with the Admiral. The place was entirely deserted and grown over with high grass.

We then sailed for this place and arrived here on the 13th.

HMS *Agincourt*, Hong Kong, November 25th, 1846

My dearest Father

Pray remember me when you write to Sir Edward and Lady Parry.

Hong Kong is very gay now. There are races on the 1st and 3rd of December and a race ball on the 4th. I have to ride a flat race on a most beautiful horse and a hurdle race on a very mere little pony.

We sail from this place the first week in December *never never* to return in the Old *Agincourt* but you must not expect to see me home until the end of May, O what a delightful time it will be.

I have a great deal of work to do getting ready for the races, exercising horses, getting jockey caps, whips &c. I am very comfortable again in the ship and get on very well with the commanding officers, and that is more than all can say.

The Governor has made himself most unpopular. He has asked me to dinner tomorrow and I did not like to refuse as I had no good excuse. The Admiral gives a grand party tomorrow also and as he generally asks me I shall be done out of a dance, and have the satisfaction of eating a pork chop and making myself unwell drinking bad wine.

You must not expect to see me grown. I am very short for my age but if I was a great big 6 foot fellow I should not be able to ride the races.

Ever my dearest Father,

one of your most affect. Sons,

S.G. Cresswell.

TWO

HMS *Investigator, 1848-1853*

Back in England in August 1847, Cresswell stayed with his mentor and friend, Sir Edward Parry, the distinguished sailor and Arctic explorer, who had penetrated as far west (starting from the eastern end) as any explorer in the Arctic seas north of Canada. Sir Edward encouraged Cresswell, now 20, to volunteer for Arctic service.

Before this phase, Cresswell was entered on the books of HMS *Victory* (having been paid off from the *Agincourt* in September), so as to be able to take six weeks leave. He went home to Lynn, the first and the last time that the whole family were together for Christmas. He then joined HMS *Excellent*, the gunnery training school in Portsmouth established in 1830. But his stay was short, and in the spring of 1848 he was appointed as a Sub-Lieutenant (then termed Mate) in HMS *Investigator*, commanded by Captain Edward Bird, on a relief and survey expedition to the Arctic. They would sail in company with HMS *Enterprise*, under the command of the Arctic veteran Sir James Ross.

The objects of the expedition were to find and give relief to the expedition of Sir John Franklin, then missing in the Arctic, and to continue the search for a North-West Passage. This goal, a navigable waterway from the Atlantic to the Pacific oceans to the north of America and Canada, continued to attract the attention of naval authorities, particularly the British, in spite of the hostile climate and extreme difficulties of navigation in the frozen north by sailing ships. Such was the commercial potential of a 'short-cut' to the East that despite the considerable cost in lives and ships, and the great hardships suffered, the Arctic sea was to be the scene of intense naval activity, especially at the eastern end nearest to Greenland.

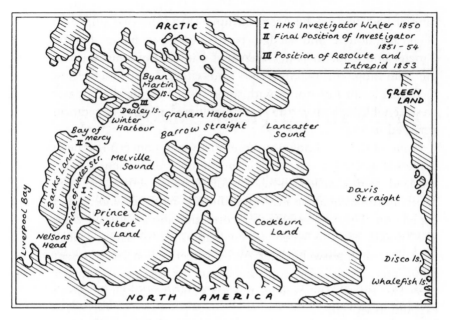

Map legend:

I HMS Investigator Winter 1850
II Final Position of Investigator 1851 – 54
III Position of Resolute and Intrepid 1853

HMS *Investigator* in the Arctic, 1850–1854.

The fascination persisted into the twentieth century. In 1969, following the discovery of rich oil deposits, near Prudhoe Bay in Northern Alaska, an American oil tanker, the *Manhattan* was equipped with a strengthened bow and sent on a trial run to see if it would be possible to ship oil from the North Slope of Alaska to the oil terminals and refineries of New Jersey on the east coast of the United States.

The attempt stalled when the tanker became trapped in the ice, and had to be rescued by an ice-breaking tug. Although the ship eventually reached its destination, the voyage was ruled a commercial failure and instead a pipe-line was constructed southward from the oil fields to the Pacific coast of Alaska. The pack ice which stopped the tanker *Manhattan* was virtually the same, and in the same place, as that which, a century earlier, trapped the Victorian sailing ships on their Arctic adventures.

The task given to Sir James Ross with *Enterprise* and *Investigator* was to find Franklin, and to bring him provisions. Sir John had left England three years earlier, in 1845 with the ships *Erebus* and *Terror*. Unknown to the Admiralty, Sir John himself had died in the Arctic in June 1847. The two ships had been abandoned and sledge parties under Captain Francis Crozier and Captain James Fitzjames had set out southward in the vain hope of making land and safety. Later discoveries, including a cairn of stones with some silver bearing the Crozier crest, established that the last members of the expedition perished in 1848.

None of this was known in London, though concern had been expressed as early as 1847, with the thought of sending a party overland from Canada to search for Franklin. His wife, Lady Franklin, was also active in urging the Admiralty to send a relief expedition. The impossibility of communication between ships like Franklin's in the Arctic and civilisation was to have a crucial influence on Cresswell's later Arctic career, when he was sent home precisely to allay concerns about the *Investigator* and her crew. This epic journey still lay five years ahead as Sir James Ross's expedition set out.

The course of *Enterprise* and *Investigator* was to pass north of Scotland and, by way of Greenland, into the Arctic. Cresswell's first letter home was written at sea off his native east coast four months before his 21st birthday.

HMS *Investigator*, at sea, May 13th, 1848

My dearest Father

I expect to send this from Yarmouth direct to you. I am quite comfortable. I hear we stay out 3 summers if we do not find Sir John, so it is most likely I shall be away 2½ years. Yesterday we were towed down into the Nore, we got under weigh this morning and are being towed along the coast with the steamer on one side and a lighter on the other hoisting in coal, 600 and odd bags and most of it has to be stowed on deck so that if possible we are in worse mess than when you came down.

There is a report that we shall put in somewhere in Scotland but I do not believe it. If we should, you may depend on hearing, or should there be any other chance.

Best love to all. Remember me truly to all the good people of Lynn,
      Ever your very Affect. Son
      S.G. Cresswell.

HMS *Investigator*, off Cromer, May 14th, 1848

Dearest Parents,

It is rather tempting being so near home,* but I am in capital pluck. We are still in tow of the tug steamer. The *Enterprise* has stopped off Yarmouth, and his steamer has gone in for coal. There is too much work to be done to make much of a Sunday of it, but I hope that by next we shall be all ship shape, that is as much as we can with 600 bags of coal and a quantity of provisions stowed on deck.

One good thing is the engineer does not mess with us, so there are only five in our mess, and capital fellows they are. The second master is rather of the rough sort but that we all shall be before we come home.

I shall send this by the pilot when he goes in. I do not expect he will leave us before we get well North. There are at this moment 150 vessels in sight from the deck.

May 16th

We cast off from the steam tug the day before yesterday in the afternoon, and a nice little air sprung up from the Southward, so we made all sail. In the evening it came on to blow rather, and we took two reefs in the topsails. We have a fine breeze today and are going 8½ knots which is tremendous going for these old tubs. I am getting my cabin into capital trim, it really looks quite stunning. The only hardship is that the little glass bull's eye is covered over by coal bags on deck, so that I have not much daylight when the door is shut.

We have not been able to get any sights yet to work the Longitude. Yesterday we were about 30 miles off the mouth of the Humber at noon.

We are pretty well on ships grub now, as we think it will best to keep the stock till we get into hard weather. I trust that you have made up your minds not to think of my return in under two years and a half, so that if I return before that it will be an agreeable surprise, and if I do not you will not be the least nervous.

We have preserved meat (pork) today, and we shall have it four days out of the seven so that we shall get on very well in the way of food.

I had the morning watch and we passed several large fishing cobs.

---

* About 40 miles as the crow flies.

HMS *Investigator*, May 18th, 1848

My dearest Parents

I fear this will be my farewell letter as the pilot leaves us tonight for good. I sent my letter in yesterday by the tug steamer that had been in company with us since we sailed. We were just off Aberdeen yesterday, now about 20 miles distant as we have had but little wind. We shall not be much to the northward of that today.

I have got all my traps stowed away in most excellent style, I have room and to spare. I have begun my private log, it will be an out and outer.

The only things I can't find among my traps are Aunt Kate's knives, but I have no doubt they will turn up. If not there are knives in the ship that will be served out as soon as we get north. I keep second in a watch at the moment, but the 1st Lieut told me the other day that as soon as we get among the ice he is going to ask the Captain to let the officers be on four watches, and for me to keep the fourth as we shall have no end of sights &c. &c. to take, and work of all sorts.

I have begun Sir J Ross's *Voyages*. Perhaps it is rather foolish to dip into the books yet, but as Anderson has offered me any of his, and he has a cabin half full, and I have no doubt the Captain will do the same when we are froze up, I shall have enough to do to get through them all.

I like the Capt. very much. He has very little to say to any body, but this is a fault on the right side, it is much better than a jawing fellow kicking up a row with all hands about nothing. He seems to me to be a thorough, practical sensible man.

I have a little youngster a messmate of mine. He is a Master Ossie Tracey by name, Son of a Lieut. that I had put under my charge. In some roundabout way I make out that Sir Edward Buxton wished me to look after him. He has been rather sea sick but is now better. He seems a very gentlemanly nice young fellow, and it will give me the greatest pleasure to help him in any way in my power.

The *Enterprise* sails a little faster than we do before the wind, but I think on a wind we have the best of it. This I think is because she is not so deep as we are, being 60 tons larger and only having the same stores and men that we have.

I suppose it is all right in a certain quarter;* if anything should happen during my absence; if she should become tired of waiting and consent

---

* I have not been able to discover the object of SGC's affections, nor did he ever marry, though evidently liking women.

become another's do not let me hear it all at once, but break the cruel news gradually as there is no saying what might be the consequences, (particularly with the Thames and London Monument so near at hand), if I heard all at one time.

We now are in Longitude 2°50'W and Latitude 50°25'N, just about 20 miles from the most northern point of Scotland. The pilot is going in.

May it please God to bless you all and so order it that we should all grow better, and with more particularly the younger part of the family, by the younger part of the family I mean all the boys, and Harriet is the prayer of your most affectionate son.

The passage of the North Atlantic took the expedition a little over five weeks, and brought the *Investigator* to landfall in Greenland, at a Danish settlement at Whale Fish Islands before the end of June 1848.

HMS *Investigator*, Whale Fish Islands, June 29th, 1848

My dearest Parents,

I believe a letter bag is to be made up to leave here, so I shall write hoping that you may get it somehow.

This is the queerest place I was ever in, nothing but a lot of small rocky barren islands, not a bit of vegetation except in one spot where the Esquimaux huts are. There is a Governor of these Islands, he is a Dane, a very queer fellow. He has a wooden house about 20 feet long and 10 wide. It has one small window and a hole in the top for the smoke to escape from. We gave him a bottle of rum, and sad to say his Excellency, forgetting his high station, got very drunk.

I cannot say that I am agreeably surprised with the Esquimaux, but they are much as I expected, filthy dirty, oily, dreadfully ugly in fact utterly disgusting in every respect. The women are a shade better than the men.

I have been trying to barter for a canoe, but you might as well ask the fellows to sell their heads. They are the most beautiful little things made of stretched seal skin, as light as a feather, about 18 feet long and about 2 feet wide, covered all over except a small hole in the middle *just* large enough for the man to sit in.

One of our marines got into one the other day, when over he went, and if he had not been near the ship, would have been drowned, as it is almost impossible to get your legs out in the water. I believe if the natives capsize they can turn up again all right.* I must say I should not like to try it.

It is very wonderful the way they throw the spear. Our ice master says he has seen them cut away a rope yarn from the fore yard, from the 2nd deck. This I do not believe although such a thing might by chance occur. There are a few seal skins, hoods, &c. &c. on show that the fellows will barter with, but I shall not have anything to do with them as they are very poor skins, and full of small animals but we won't say what.

I have had some capital shooting, I have shot several duck *all flying* and a good many other birds. The sun never sets now, it does not go near the horizon by several degrees. The best time for shooting is from 7 at night to 2 in the morning.

Last night we, that is Anderson, Barnard (who by the by has turned out a capital fellow, in fact it would not go down any body being any thing but a good fellow in this ship), and Addams the Asst. Surgeon, and myself, 4 of us went away from the ship at 5 and returned at 12.30 having shot 12 duck. I shot 2 and had a share in two more. The Captain was away in another place and shot 7. The day before yesterday the Capt. shot 5, Sir J Ross 6. The day before that 22 were shot, 12 by us and 10 by *Enterprise*. We have shot upwards of 40 duck since we have been here, and lots of other birds.

I have got the credit of being a dab shot. A few days before we got in here we got our guns, rifles &c. up to try them. A bottle was hung up forward and the Captain and all the fellows were blazing away (with ball of course) and could not hit it. I then went down and got my gun, came up and knocked it over first shot, another was put up and I broke him, and then another and I served him likewise, three running. All the officers looked at me as if I was a regular stormer.

I should then have marched below, covered by my glory, but ambition almost ruined me. The next two shots I missed and the Capt. made the remark 'See you were very well at first but you can't hit it now.' There was a last bottle, I now hung up. I made a careful shot, and smash it went, so that I hit 4 out of 6 shots, and the Capt. did not hit once out of about 20.

---

* To this day the manoeuvre is known to canoeists as an 'Eskimo roll'.

I do not suppose it will hurt the gun firing ball out of it with a small charge. The ducks here are immensely large. One I shot the other day weighed more than 7 lbs and they are all about that weight. The weight of a goose in England is about 8, we have not seen one goose or swan.

I shot the most lovely little water bird the other day, not much bigger than a sparrow, but of course it was bound for a specimen for Government, as all things will be that we shoot or find. But I could not stuff them if I had them, and if I could I have not an inch of room to stow them in.

We live off the fat of the land here, birds and eggs of all sorts all goes down. The scientific men have been making no end of observations, a whole lot of dodges to find the dip of the needle &c. I not being a scientificer do not understand much about it.

I have not been idle since we left. In the navigation way I have worked a good deal, and after we leave here shall work much harder when I get to sea again.

The weather is most lovely, quite hot, the thermometer up nearly to 60 and as high as 70 in the sun. We have hardly had a drop of rain since we left England. I bathed here the other day. The water was dreadfully cold. All the tips of the high hills of Disco Island are covered with snow, and there is a good deal about here not yet thawed, but it is thawing fast.

The other day I went to the top of a hill and counted 130 icebergs in sight. Every now and then an iceberg splits and sounds like the firing of heavy guns.

I think, in fact I am sure, that the most beautiful sight I ever saw was as we were running in for the land. It was my middle watch, a thick fog. About two, the fog rose like a curtain, and there was Disco, the sun lighting up the hills, the valleys looking like gold. I have often seen gold sky but never land before. This wonderful light, together with the black rocks, white snow, and sea studded with icebergs, some immense, was the most, unearthly'ly splendid thing I ever saw or ever expect to see.

We fell in with the first ice about 150 miles South East of Cape Farewell. We had to keep away for some miles to clear it. It was a field of ice, and very wonderful it was to see a floating field in the middle of the sea so far from any land. We fell in with the first iceberg soon after entering Davis' Straight, and since then have seen numbers of them, some very large. We have not been once obliged to alter out course more than a few hundred yards on account of ice, but we must expect soon to be amongst it pretty thick after we leave here.

The Esquimaux tell us that they had a very hard winter and would all have starved if it had not been for a whale they caught last summer, and this kept them in food. Fancy the Lynn people being kept alive by the whale that was caught when they had to screw their courage up to stand the smell but for a few minutes; and here, in another part of the world people are too glad to keep it, stinking as it is, and live off it.

We have not got a word of information about Sir J Franklin further than is known in England. We have been here a week today, we sail tonight I believe, or tomorrow morning. I have taken great pains with my drawing since I have been away and the more I try to draw, the more I am sure I have no taste for it. I will do my best.

I shall not be able to do much in the painting line as I have not got any indigo with me, the most important colour possible, and the only person in the ship that has is the Asst. Surveyor, but as he has but one cake which will be barely enough for him while we are out, I cannot get a rub.

P.S. Perhaps you will like to hear what I am reading. I am in the middle of my dearest Grandmother's* life. I think it does me a great deal of good. May we all be enabled to follow as near as possible in her holy steps. That all can be as good as she was is impossible. We are not all given 5 talents, but if we have but one, it is no reason that we should hide it in the sand.

In the second place I am reading the History of British India. I have read a good deal since I have been away, and have got books enough to last me for years as I have the use of those in the Capt's cabin, the ship's library &c. &c.

HMS *Investigator*, Upernavik Womans Isles, Baffin Bay,
Lat 72°47'N Long 56°40'W, July 12th, 1848

My dearest Parents

We sailed from Whale Fish Islands on the 30th of June.

The sea was very clear of ice, this, with the information that Esquimaux gave us at Whale Fish Islands about the hard winter made us think that the ice could not be much broken up to the Northwards, as if it had, we should have more, and we have found such to be the case.

---

* Elizabeth Fry.

On the 3rd of July about 8 in the morning we observed the ice in a long line ahead as far as the eye could reach both on the starboard and port bow. The wind was against us, so we tacked before we came to the ice, and stood on the other from the ice toward the Eastern shore. The winds have been very light, we twice have had all boats down to tow.

On July 5th five Whalers hove in sight. Standing out from the land four of them came and communicated with us. I believe that all the information that we got from them was that we should not be able to get further, or not more than 30 miles further to the Northward, that they have not been further to the Northward. Most of them had got four fish which is considered very fair, having no news of any sort about Sir John Franklin.

The following are the names of the Whalers, as you most likely will hear of their arrival in England: *True Love, Alexander, Lady Jane* and *Joseph Green*. I sent a letter by the *True Love*. It was a very miserable one, but I was sure that any would be better than none.

On the 7th we made fast to an iceberg, nearly losing a boat, and boat's crew.

The 2nd Master, and six hands were sent to lay out an ice anchor to a berg about a mile from the ship. They got to the berg all right, but as the side nearest the ship was very high and perpendicular, were obliged to go round the other side to land the men. Three landed, the boat then returned to the face of the iceberg, the men walking to the top, and sending down a lead line to the boat to haul the ice anchor up by. The anchor was no sooner bent on, than crack went the iceberg.

The next thing that any body knows of the matter is that they were half full of water in the boat, all wet through, laying about in different parts of the boat.

The 2nd Master was somewhere forward, with the boatswain's mate that was pulling the stroke oar on the top of him, and all bruised more or less. On looking round they found the boat was some way from the iceberg, that she was surrounded with ice and boiling water, that the old quarter-master that had been on the iceberg, nearly 60 feet high, was comfortably floating on a piece of ice about a stone's throw from the berg, the driest of the party, and the other two men were safe on the berg.

I think it was the most wonderful escape I have ever seen. Just think that it was not soft snow but ice, as hard as a rock and that tons of it fell from a height of 50 feet when the boat was but a yard or two from the berg and immediately under the place where it came down. How she escaped seems to me and those in the boat, a perfect miracle, and how the quarter-master had his flying trip without breaking his neck or being thrown off I rate as another.

I was standing on the deck at the time, watching the boat. I saw the ice break away and fall, I turned away and said 'Oh God, they are all lost' the next moment I saw the boat floating, I hardly could believe my eyes for the first moment. It came down like the roar of very heavy guns.

But I must not feast you on the dangers, or you will fancy that we are always playing with danger.

This is a very snug place, and as we can't get any further to the north yet, on account of the ice not having broken up, we must make ourselves very jolly here. There is a settlement of Esquimaux and 9 Danes here. They are a little shade cleaner than the Whale Fish Island fellows, but are dirty enough. You need be quite happy about my bringing you home a Esquimaux daughter-in-law. The shooting is No 1 here, but it is such murder I am almost sick of it.

The other night five of us shot 5 duck, a magnificent gull 5ft 6½ ins from tip to tip of wing, and 94 loons. Shooting the loons is the thing I do not like, the poor things, many of them on their eggs. They swarm in one place under a cliff that is 2,000 feet high, and actually sit to be shot. They fly away as soon as the gun is fired, but come back again immediately after. They are very good eating, much nicer than the duck which are very fishy.

Yesterday I was sent away with a shooting party of men, we shot 73; the Captain his boat 45, Sir J Ross in his 66, and another boat of our men in charge of the 2nd Master 48, making a grand total of 232 birds, chiefly loons in one night. My gun behaves capitally.

The loon is a pretty bird, a sort of diver of about 2 lbs weight. We have got enough game on board to feed the ship's company for days.

I believe we leave here tomorrow to try and get a little further to the northward. The thing that we want chiefly is a strong northerly wind to clear away the ice.

I need not repeat that I am very happy and comfortable. You will understand that there is not a chance of our being back this year, the ice being in such a fixed state.

There are yet one or two whalers to the northward, all the rest have gone south.

The weather is beautiful. I do not dislike the everlasting day, the sun never setting by a long way. I must say I should rather like to see a star again, however we shall see enough of them in the winter to make up for the lack of them now.

P.S. The iceberg that we have made fast to has just split, with a great crash but fortunately has not hurt either ship. One of the *Enterprise*'s men that was on it was thrown off into the water, but only got a cold bath as he was soon picked up.

P.P.S. All our men are in capital health, no one in the lists in both ships.

As it turned out, the expedition made no further progress owing largely to the thickness of the ice, from the previous hard winter. This had prevented the usual breaking up of the ice to allow navigation towards the area of the Great Fish River where, had they known it, the remnants of Franklin's party perished. Sir James Ross led a land party from the ships on North Somerset Island, a land-mass to the west of Greenland, not far from the Great Fish River, but they neither found any traces, nor heard any word of the travellers from the Esquimaux or whalers. The ships overwintered at Cape Leopold, solidly frozen in, with ice and snow cover, not unlike igloo vessels and at no hazard from the elements.

HMS *Investigator* [Undated, Autumn 1849]

My dearest Parents,

Thank God I am once more in old England. To write a long letter I cannot. It may seem an odd thing to say after having been eighteen months away, but I think you will understand my feelings. One thing I can say is that I am perfectly well, and only wait for *good* news from home to be perfectly happy.

We have *not* discovered a trace of Sir John Franklin or any of his party. I fear they have all perished.

P.S. Pray send my plain clothes to me by the first chance as I have nothing to go on shore in.

Cresswell's conclusion about the Franklin expedition did not, however, bring to an end the Admiralty's interest in the Arctic sea. Within only a few weeks it was determined that the *Investigator* and *Enterprise* should once more set out to continue the search for the North-West Passage, and any traces of Franklin's expedition.

For the new expedition *Investigator* was to be commanded by a new skipper, Captain Robert M'Clure, and a new route was to be attempted. *Enterprise* and *Investigator* were ordered to proceed southward across the Atlantic, and, via the Straits of Magellan into the Pacific Ocean.

The course of the two ships lay via the Sandwich Islands (now Hawaii) to provision, and north to the Bering Strait, where they would turn eastward into the Arctic sea. A steamer, HMSV *Gorgon* was also despatched to help the two sailing ships round Cape Horn. However, in the event, the *Gorgon* was unequal to the task of towing the ships together, and amid some confusion, the *Enterprise* and *Investigator* became separated as each entered the Pacific Ocean.

Thereafter, although the crew of the *Investigator* had occasional reports of the *Enterprise*, the two ships never sailed in company again. In the event, *Enterprise* arrived too late in the year to enter the Arctic sea, and postponed her voyage for a year, wintering in Hong Kong. *Investigator* was, from May 1850, on her own.

HMS *Investigator*, Sunday [January 1850]

My dearest Parents,

We are now about 8 miles from the North Foreland, towing with wind and tide against us. I shall send this in with the pilot who leaves us at the Downs. The Capt. continues to be very civil to me but poor Haswell catches it on all occasions. Yesterday the Capt. went on in a most foolish way with him, saying that he should not be in his ship and that he was incompetant to be 1st Lieutenant, and that he would write to I do not know who about him.

Now this is too bad particularly as Haswell is ten thousand times more of an officer and a sailor than our worthy Captain ever was or ever will be. Haswell would have had a row with the Capt. yesterday about his unreasonable conduct to him, but he is determined to put all he possibly can in his pipe and smoke it, as the saying is.

I like all my *messmates* very much, and I think we will be very comfortable notwithstanding our Chief. We are getting on putting things to rights. Our Mess place will be very comfortable.

Three of our men ran at Greenhithe, we are now 7 short of complement. I had the middle watch last night. It is rather disgusting having to turn out to keep watch after having been for some time in snug quarters on shore, but turning in after your watch is so jolly that it almost makes up for the bore of turning out.

HMS *Investigator*, at sea, Thursday

My dear Joe,*

I write a line to you to send when we get into Plymouth which will be in a few hours. We hove to yesterday at 5 P.M., as we did not think it prudent to run for Plymouth in the dusk as it was blowing a very strong gale. At 8 o'clock it blew tremendously; we were laying to under main trysail. Everything else was furled. Such work, all sorts of things flying about the decks in all directions, casks fetching away &c. &c. It was my morning watch and I can assure you I was not sorry to see daylight and the wind more moderate. We bore up this morning, 8 o'clock and made sail, 3 reefs in the topsails & foresail at 8.30.

The *Enterprise* hove in sight on the port bow we having lost her since rounding the North Foreland.

The Capt. has put such a rum little 'mid' in my watch, in the shape of our poor old ice mate, a man that has been to sea for the last 20 years. I would rather have been without him, as I should think he would not like to be under such a comparative youngster as myself, but I will try and make it as comfortable as I can for him.

We passed a small pilot boat last night just before the gale came on. She must have been out in the whole of it (about 19 tons). It was bitterly cold, and has been since we left the river.

There has not been an open rupture between the Capt. and 1st Lieut. for a day or two, only a little gentle bullying &c. He still continues very civil to me, I think he is waiting until we leave England. I do not care a pin about him so you need not make yourself unhappy about my being uncomfortable.

---

* His brother, Joseph Cresswell.

My cabin was in a most awful state last night, books, candles, coffee, tooth powder &c. &c. &c . . . flying about in all directions.

HMS *Investigator*, Plymouth Sound, January 17th, 1850
My Dearest Father

Two of the men that ran* at Greenhithe have joined here . . .

I fear that we shall not sail before Saturday or Sunday as we can't get our preserved meats from Ireland.

The more I see of Armstrong the more I think him a good fellow of the first water and also Haswell. The rest of my messmates I like very much, and I think we shall be very comfortable.

HMS *Investigator*, Plymouth Sound, January 18th, 1850
My dearest Parents

Will you be so good as to see that Mr Dennis is paid. I have not paid him but left it to you, as John gave me the sounding sextant.

We have got half a gale of wind from the South westward. This is a very great bore as it will be impossible to sail with it in such tubs† as these. We have got about ¼ of our preserved meats on board, the rest have not yet arrived from Ireland. I have no news since yesterday. Three of our men ran last night, it was a very foolish thing paying them their six months in advance before leaving Greenhithe. Poor Haswell has 5 sisters living here and as far as I can make out he supports them.

HMS *Investigator*, Plymouth Sound, Saturday Jan 19th, 11 O'clock P.M.
My dearest Parents

This will be the last chance of writing as we sail the first thing in the morning. I have nothing to say except that I shall not forget to pray that God may bless and keep you my dearest parents and grant that we may

---

* ran = deserted.

† Commander Sherard Osborn, naval colleague, friend of Cresswell, and author of *The Discovery of North-West Passage* (Longmans 1856), gives this account of the appearence of the *Investigator*: 'A water washed looking vessel of barely 400 tons register . . . Everything in the shape of outward ornament carefully eschewed, a solemn coating of black paint, but little relieved by a white riband and small figurehead, added to the appearence of strength and weight of the little, but I am afraid I cannot say *pretty* vessel.'

live to meet again in this world, but if God should think fit to order things otherwise that he may lead us one by one to his glorious throne to meet our dearest lost ones in glory everlasting.

I have been obliged to draw £15 on my account at Lynn as there were sudden little things I found out I wanted on the way down, and our mess has proved more expensive than we expected. We have £580 of mess stock on board. Will you be so good as to send Bill £1 from me, and put it down to my account, and pay the enclosed bill by post office order.

I get on as yet very well with the Capt. and think I shall. We are *most* comfortable in our mess.

This was the last letter from Cresswell until *Investigator* was in the north Pacific ocean, on the point of entering the Arctic. However, a detailed account of the voyage of the *Investigator* is available in the diary of Johann August Miertsching, a Moravian Baptist missionary who was taken on the voyage as an Esquimaux interpreter. The following brief extracts from his journal carry *Investigator* on the first part of her journey.

Sunday, January 20th, 1850

Our ship, the *Investigator* is of 423 tons with three masts. The crew consists of 66 sailors: Captain, Robert LeMesurier M'Clure; two Lieutenants, Haswell and S.G.Cresswell; two mates (sub-lieutenants), R. Wynniatt and H. Sainsbury; two ship's doctors, Dr. Armstrong and H. Piers; J.C. Paine, ship's clerk in charge of supplies; S. Court, sailing master. Also Mr Newton, ice-master. These officers are called wardroom or gunroom officers.

The men are divided into three classes. The first class are petty officers to which four artisans, armourer, breadmaker, cook, sailmaker, etc., belong. The Captain has a cook and two stewards, the officers the same. The sailors on the lower deck – where they sleep in hammocks – are divided into messes, 8 men to a mess. Each officer sleeps in his own cabin, seven feet square, with bed, washstand, desk and chair. Each officer has a servant who keeps his cabin in order, does his washing and mending, etc.

As on our ship there are no boys, the eight marines, one corporal and one sergeant are appointed as servants, and for that receive twelve shillings a month in addition to their regular pay. Of cannon we have only two pieces, but a large stock of muskets, pistols, hand grenades and rockets. Rations consist of salt beef and pork, fresh boiled beef and veal; vegetables are beans, dried cabbage, and meal. At breakfast, cocoa, at night, tea with biscuit. Vinegar, pickles, mustard etc., are served twice weekly. Before our ship left England the officers pooled £450 sterling, and purchased with it wine, beer and a variety of foods.

The day is divided into four-hour watches; each watch consisting of an officer and fifteen to twenty men, is on duty for four hours; and this rotation is kept up day and night.

At 5 a.m. the reveille sounds; the interior of the ship is cleaned throughout and everything well polished; at 8 is breakfast; at 9 a general muster on the foredeck at which every man must appear; until 11.30 the sailors are usefully employed; at 12 the midday meal; until 1.30 the men are free, then work until 5; at 6 tea and until 8 p.m. the men are expected to take part in sport. At 8 o'clock to bed. The officers dine at 2p.m., the Captain at 4. The officers sleep when they please. Each day at noon rations are issued for the ensuing day to the various messes by the officer in charge of stores. The daily grog ration is one gill per man.

February 24th, 1850

Each Sunday there is Divine service; the Captain stands and reads from the Prayer Book, a psalm, two chapters from the Bible, the Ten Commandments and the Gospel and Epistle prescribed for that Sunday.

March 12th, 1850

Fine wind and weather; several ships seen; forty English miles from the Brazilian coast; flying fish swarm around the ship. In the evening from 6 to 8 a grand spectacle, dramatics and dancing.

April 6th, 1850

Of the four men under arrest one today was given four dozen lashes on the back with the cat-and-nine-tails.

April 15th, 1850

In the morning land close aboard, Cape Virgin! Thousands of great white birds seen on the beach. Mr Cresswell shot a white swan. Ten a.m. at the entrance of the Straits of Magellan. To the right the land of

Patagonia, to the left Tierra del Fuego. On the green hills we saw grazing great herds of llamas. Here are no trees, only low bushes.

It was at this point that the two ships were assisted by HMSV *Gorgon* to make the passage to the Pacific Ocean. In the event, they became separated. On arrival at Port Famine, on the Chilean shore, *Investigator* found that *Enterprise* had already passed, and what is more taken with her all the bullocks available there, so that *Investigator's* crew would have to go without fresh meat until they arrived at the Sandwich Islands.

Investigator made a good passage up the Pacific, notwithstanding encountering the severe weather common to the southern seas. Miertsching's diary continues:

May 10th, 1850

Wind and weather very unfavourable: for the last fourteen days we have been able to carry only two small sails in the gale and heavy seas. The bulwarks are smashed; there is much water in the ship, and the cabins and everything are drenched; fourteen seamen lie sick below. I caught a large bird, an albatross,* fifteen pound in weight, the wings ten feet five inches. The waves often deluge the upper deck and leave behind small fish and other creatures of the sea.

June 29th, 1850

Until now always magnificent weather and fair wind. As we shall now soon be in the Sandwich Islands, drinking water is now being issued without restriction. Most of the salt pork, cheese, smoked meat etc., in the ship has been spoiled by dampness and heat . . . Each evening I am with the Captain on the quarter-deck until 11 p.m.; it is the pleasantest part of the day. The ship is repainted and all the damage wrought by the waves repaired. Nine men are still sick. Frequently the Captain grants the men an extra grog.

---

* Coleridge's 'Rime of the Ancient Mariner' seems to have been responsible for the myth that seamen regarded the killing of albatrosses as unlucky: before the poem became common currency, albatross-hunting was a popular seaman's pursuit.

July 21st, 1850

Weather very foggy; strong south-west wind. In the afternoon in 137 fathoms depth. Countless sea-fowl around the ship; every one known to me from Labrador. In the evening steering for Unalaska where the captain wishes to buy fresh meat from the Russian traders.

Cresswell now briefly takes up the story:

HMS *Investigator*, off Flaxman Is., August 21st, 1850

My dearest parents

I write this on the faint chance that it one day may reach you . . .

On the 31st of July we met the *Herald* off Cape Lisborne* finding the *Enterprise* had not been there, or if she had, not seen. Captain Kellett came on board – he is a fine old fellow – but wished to detain us for a few days to see if the *Enterprise* would come up. He hardly could believe we only left the Sandwich Islands on the 2nd of the month, he would have it at first that we must mean the 2nd of June instead of July.

Captain M'Clure was very strong for pushing on, telling Capt. Kellett that if he liked to detain him he could, but at the same time he must take the responsibility, that as far as he was concerned he would get on. Nearly all that day we were drawing stores from the *Herald*. We also got 3 *good* men that we were short, hearty good wishes and cheers.

It was the Capt.'s intention to have landed these letters at Cape Bathurst. As we are some distance off in a foul wind I did not hurry my despatch. Natives are now seen on shore, and if this proves to be an encampment we shall land the letters here in a very short time.

We rounded Point Barrow on the 6th of August not without some difficulty and danger, a foul wind and tremendous ice, but we had luck or a merciful providence taking care of us, and in the morning the wind became fair and we made for the land. In the forenoon the wind died away. We could see open water extending about 5 miles from the low land. We were about 2 miles from the water, it took us all day to get to it.

---

* On the north-west shore of the Bering Strait. Flaxman Island was to the east along the north coast of Alaska between Point Barrow and the Mackenzie River. Liverpool Bay, whence this letter was sent, lies further to the east, on the Canadian, rather than Alaskan coast.

The Esquimaux are a good tempered laughing, thriving people, but Oh so dirty. I believe they never wash from the day they are born to the time they go to the last long home. We made them some presents and got some bows and arrows in exchange.

It is most curious, the custom of rubbing noses. I bent on those at our island where there were a good many rather cleaner than the general run, and managed to pick a clean chief to operate on.

We have been twice on shore, and on one of the occasions, having hoisted out provisions to lighten ship, one of the boats upset and we lost 11 casks of salt beef, about a year's salt beef. But we only get it once a week, so it is only two month's actual meat.

The other day we ran 70 miles off shore into the pack, but we were very glad to get out of it again and I think it is doubtful if it might not have proved our winter quarters if we had not had a fine commanding breeze to run in shore with. We now are off Cape Warren.

To get here we have had a good many difficulties to surmount, but not more than is generally attendant on Arctic cruising. I do not think it is impossible that we may make the North-West Passage if the Capt. will but keep to the land. I am sure it is the only way to navigate a Polar sea. This is not an original opinion, it was Parry's and Sir James Ross's and is I believe our own Captain's, or he says so.

But if he sees open water, he has not strength of mind to keep from running into it. We should have been at Cape Bathurst, but we were obliged to stand off shore, the wind blowing E.N.E. and made the ice on the 2nd of August at daylight, or rather about 4 o'clock as there was no dark, the sun not setting.

There have been no chances of sending letters except the *Herald*. If this should find its way to England you will at the same time get Capt. M'Clure's despatch, pray keep it for me. It will be a most egotistical production, mark my words for it.

It is quite impossible to say where the *Enterprise* may be. Poor Collinson, I half fear that he will go mad when he hears the slow sailing *Investigator* has passed him. Pray tell Sir Edward Parry the news. It is well I did not attempt to give you the whereabouts of our winter quarters. I can't, it will wholly depend on circumstances.

The Captain says we shall try and push North after leaving Cape Bathurst, but as he alters his mind half a dozen times a day it is impossible to say. We all fraternize mostly well, altho' I do not like him, but better than I did at the time of our most deadly war.

To tell you my dearest parents how often I think of you all, how often I hope that Frank has quite got round again, and how I long to hear of all your welfare, is more than I have time to do, with best love to all,

Lat. 69°47'N Long. 131°35'W, August 24th

I am well, happy and comfortable, but you will see this by the tenor of my letter.

HMS *Investigator*, Liverpool Bay, near Cape Bathurst, August 30th, 1850

I open this to give you a later look at my welfare. We have not made much progress as you will see since the 24th, nothing but foul winds, and some very light, so much so that having a current against us we have made a retrograde progress. But all this easterly wind may be good for us, it must clear the land to the eastward of us of ice. I much fear you will never get this. Should you get it, best love to all.

This was Cresswell's last letter home, and the last his family and friends, or his masters at the Admiralty heard from the expedition for three years and one month.

But the progress of the *Investigator* and her crew was recorded not only in Johann Miertsching's journal, but also by Captain M'Clure, and, later, in a journal kept by Cresswell himself. Sherard Osborn used much of this material, and had many conversations with Cresswell and M'Clure when writing his account of the voyage, *The Discovery of the North-West Passage* published by Longmans in 1856.

Cresswell's journal records his overland journey with sick crewmen from the *Investigator* to comparative safety on board HMS *Resolute*, under the command of Captain Henry Kellet in the spring of 1853. The same Captain Kellet had been in command of the *Herald* in 1850, the last ship seen by the *Investigator* before her entry into the Arctic ice. Captain Kellet thus witnessed both the start and the finish of Cresswell and his colleagues' traverse of the North-West Passage.

Using the various sources, M'Clure, Miertsching, Cresswell and Sherard Osborn, I have pieced together the story of the epic crossing of the North-West Passage by boat, sledge and on foot. Many dramatic episodes emerged when all was over, and the survivors of HMS *Investigator*, the *'Investigators'* as they were familiarly known, eventually returned to England.

In what follows, I give the date, and authorship of the accounts, concentrating on what Cresswell experienced and witnessed, even when told by others.

Capt. M'Clure:

[September 6th, 1850]

First sight of land to the north after entering the Arctic:

At four A.M. upon the morning of 6th September, 1850, we were off the small islands near Cape Parry bearing N.E. by N., with a fine westerley breeze, and loose sailing ice, interspersed with many heavy floe pieces; the main pack was about three miles to the N.W., apparently one solid mass.

At 11.30 A.M. high land was observed on the port bow, bearing N.E. by N., distant about 50 miles. On approaching it, the main pack appeared to be resting upon the western shore, which side it was my intention to have coasted, had it been possible; the eastern one being, however, comparatively clear, as far as could be ascertained from the masthead, decided me to follow the water, supposing it an island round which a passage would be found into the Polar Sea. We shortly after hove to, and, with the first whale-boat and cutter, landed and took possession, in the name of Her Most Gracious Majesty, Calling it 'Baring's Island', in honour of the First Lord of the Admiralty.

A pole was erected, with a large painted ball upon it, near which a cask was left, containing a notification and other particulars of our having been there. The sights obtained by artificial horizon place the signal staff in Lat 71°6'N.; Long. 123°0'W., and the fall of the tide was ascertained to be six inches during one hour and a half.

We observed numerous recent traces of reindeer, hare, and wild fowl; moss and divers species of wild flowers were also in great abundance; many specimens of them, equally, as of other subjects of interest to the naturalist, were selected with much care by Dr. Armstrong.

From an elevation obtained of about 500 feet, we had a fine view toward the interior, which was well clothed with moss, giving a verdant appearence to the ranges of hills that rose gradually to between 2,000 and 3,000 feet, intersected with ravines, which must convey a copious supply of water to a large lake situated in the centre of a wide plain, about 15 miles distant.

[September 7th, 1850]

We continued working to windward the whole of the night, and by 9.30 A.M. of the 7th of September were off the South Cape, a fine bold headland, the cliffs rising perpendicularly upwards of a thousand feet, which was named 'Lord Nelson's Head' in memory of the hero whose early career was connected with Arctic adventure.

[October 8th, 1850]

At six A.M. of the 17th of September, the wind which had been light from the N.W. gradually died away, when we were almost immediately beset. There were several heavy floes in the vicinity; one, full six miles in length passed at the rate of two knots, crushing everything impeding its progress, and grazed our starboard bow.

Fortunately there was but young ice upon the opposite side, which yielded to the pressure; had it otherwise occurred, the vessel must inevitably have been cut assunder. In the afternoon we secured to a moderate sized piece, drawing eight fathoms, which appeared to offer a fair refuge, and from which we never afterwards parted; it conveyed us to our farthest N.E. position, Lat 73°7'N.; Long 117°10'W.; back round the Princess Royal Islands. Passed the largest within 500 yards, in Lat 72°42'N., Long 118°42'W.; returning along the coast of Prince Albert's Land, and finally freezing in at Lat 72°50'N.; Long 117°55'W.; upon the 30th of September, during which circumnavigation we received many severe nips, and were frequently driven close to the shore, from which our deep friend kept us off. To avoid separation we had secured with two stream-cables (one chain), two six and two five-inch hawsers. As our exposed position rendered every precaution necessary, we got upon deck 12 months' provisions, with tents, warm clothing &c., and issued to each person a pair of carpet boots and blanket bag; so that, in the event of any emergency making it imperative to quit the vessel, we might not be destitute. On the 8th of October our perplexities terminated with a nip, that lifted the vessel a foot, and heeled her thirty degrees to port, in consequence of a large tongue getting beneath her, in which position we quietly remained.

This was to be the first winter quarters of the *Investigator* in the Arctic, towards the northern end of the channel running northeast-southwest between Banks' Land to the north, and Prince Albert Land to the south.

Having come so far, and with such a momentous end to their journey, Captain M'Clure wasted little time establishing that the Prince of Wales Strait did reach the open water of Melville Sound. This link confirmed the object of their journey, a North-West Passage between Atlantic and Pacific Oceans.

Sir Edward Parry sailing from the west had penetrated as far as the southwestern tip of Melville Island, on the north shore of Melville Sound, in 1820, with his ships *Hecla* and *Griper*. If Captain M'Clure, coming from the east found that the Prince of Wales Strait reached the open water, then the circle was completed, the North-West Passage established.

Osborn:

[October 1850]

October the 21st, 1850 came in with a temperature ranging a little below zero, light winds and an overcast sky. The ice of the strait appeared to have remained stationary during the last spring tides, and the usual Polar accompaniment of strong gales. Captain M'Clure therefore determined to start for Barrow's Strait with a sledge party manned with six men . . . Hearty were the cheers, and 'Well fare ye!'s on either side as the little sledge party bade good-bye to ship and companions, and plodded on their lonely way, to bring back one day to their ship-mates the most interesting intelligence ever told to the hundreds who have devoted health, strength and energy to the problem of a North-West Passage.

The headlong zeal of the excited crew upon the sledge soon received a lesson of patience from the rugged and broken pack [ice], by the frequent capsizing of the sledge, and its eventual fracture beyond all repair. There was nothing then for it but to send back to the ship for another sledge while the rest pitched the tent, and slept their first night under canvas upon the frozen ocean.

At the close of the first day's journey the truly frugal meal of Captain M'Clure and his men was a pint of tepid water apiece into which a little oatmeal was thrown . . .

The next day the men again had tepid water, but this time flavoured (or strengthened) with chocolate. So they proceeded over ice sometimes hummocky, sometimes smooth, for another two days. On the 24th of October, M'Clure walked on ahead to spy out the land, and returned with the estimate that, from a hill 12 miles away, they would be able to see the open water of what was then known as Barrow's Strait, now re-named M'Clure Sound in his honour.

Every man now dragged with a will, in the hope of reaching that night the end of their journey; but after seven hours' toilsome labour, the tantalising cape still retained its original position . . .

Captain M'Clure then saw that he had been much deceived in its apparent distance, owing to the clearness of the atmosphere, and that thirty miles was a nearer estimate . . .

After a night's rest and another hard day's work, they were still two miles off the cape . . . Away to the north-east they already saw that wonderful oceanic ice which Sir Edward Parry so well described in his memorable voyage to Melville Island . . . Great hills and dales of blue crystalline sea ice rolled on before them in the direction of Melville Island.

The morning of the 26th of October, 1850, was fine and cloudless; it was with no ordinary feelings of joy and gratitude that Captain M'Clure and his party started before sunrise to obtain from the adjacent hill a view of that sea which connected their discoveries with those of Sir Edward Parry. Ascending a hill 600 feet above the sea level, they patiently awaited the increase of light to reveal the long-sought-for North-West Passage . . .

As the sun rose the panorama slowly unveiled itself . . .

Raised as they were at an altitude of 600 feet, the eyesight embraced a distance which precluded the possibility of any land lying between them and Melville Island. The North-West Passage was discovered!

Now, Commander Osborn drily remarks, 'it alone remained for Captain M'Clure, his officers and men to perfect the work by traversing the few thousand miles of known ground between them and their homes.' For Cresswell, the first of them to return, the journey took three weeks less than three years to achieve.

The immediate aftermath of the discovery of the Passage was dramatic enough. The temperature was dropping rapidly and M'Clure was anxious to get back to the ship and end the trials of the sledge party: 'Their fur robes were frozen into a solid mass, which could only be thawed by the men lying on them for some hours; the blanket bags were so stiff from the same cause as to stand erect; and their clothes, caps, whiskers and beards were frozen together, and required to be thawed inside the tent after they had retired to rest; and when the clothes were taken off, they had to be placed under the body that they might not freeze again: and the hardships and discomforts to be endured in consequence of the lateness of the season, although no novelty to the Arctic traveller, would appear almost fabulous to others if minutely described.'

The party hurried on towards the ship, and the Captain had something of a scare on the way: 'On the 30th October, at 2 pm, having seen the Princess Royal Isles, and knowing the position of the *Investigator* from them, Captain M'Clure left the sledge, with the intention of pushing for the ship, and having a warm meal ready for his men on their arrival'.

This generous impulse turned out badly, as, six miles from the ship, nightfall and a thick mist overtook M'Clure, and in spite of firing both barrels of his gun to attract attention, he was not found, and was obliged to spend the night on the ice: 'It was now', M'Clure recounts, 'half past eight. There were eleven hours of night before me, a temperature 15 degrees below zero, bears prowling about, and I with an unloaded gun in my hands . . .'

'I walked to and fro upon my hummock until I suppose it must have been eleven o'clock. . . .' when he gave up hope of a search party from the ship to find him.

'Descending from the top of the slab of ice upon which I had clambered, I found under its lee a famous bed of soft dry snow, and thoroughly tired out I threw myself upon it and slept for perhaps three hours, when upon opening my eyes I fancied I saw the flash of a rocket. Jumping upon my feet, I found that the mist had cleared off and that the stars and aurora-borealis were shining in all the splendour of an Arctic night.'

Sunrise enabled him to find the ship the next morning, 31 October, and the remainder of the sledge party soon arrived.

Meanwhile those remaining on the ship had been preparing for the winter which was about to set in with the setting of the Arctic sun for eleven weeks on 11 November. A shooting party secured a fine herd of musk oxen, consisting, Osborn says, of three bulls, a cow, and a calf, yielding a supply of 1,296 lbs of meat. 'The moral effect of the fact that such a quantity of fresh food could be found near a place where they were frozen up until it pleased Providence to release them, was very beneficial on the minds of all . . .'

'The ventilating tubes to the lower deck were now fitted, to force out by a current of pure but cold air the heated and deleterious vapour generated between decks by a number of men living in so confined a space. The last winter housings were spread, and a winter school-room established, to which thirty pupils immediately repaired to learn to read and write'.

So began the winter of 1850-51, with the ship's crew established in habitable conditions, and the prospects of progress good when the ice should retreat in the spring, and further exploration be possible.

In May and June of 1851, Cresswell led two parties away from the *Investigator* to survey the coasts of Bank's Land. During the summer, when the ice had melted to free the ship from her winter position, Captain M'Clure took the *Investigator* west and south to try by passing to the north of Bank's Land to make further progress from the northeast shore in an easterly direction towards Melville Island. In the event, *Investigator* did not complete the passage round Bank's Land, but after an extraordinary ice-passage including remarkable adventures arrived at a safe anchorage for the next, and succeeding winters.

M'Clure:

[August 20th, 1851]

Upon the morning of the 19th of August, 1851, we passed between two small islands, lying at the entrance of what appeared a deep inlet, running E.S.E., and then turning sharp to the N.E. It had a barrier of ice extending across, which prevented any examination.

Wishing to keep between the northernmost of these islands and the mainland, to avoid the pack which was very near it, we narrowly escaped getting on shore, as a reef extended from the latter to within half a mile of the island. Fortunately, the wind being light, we rounded to with all the studding sails set, and let go the anchor in 2½ fathoms, having about four inches to spare under the keel, and warped into four fathoms, while Mr Court was sent to find a channel; in which he succeeded, carrying three fathoms, through which we ran for one mile, and then continued our course in eight, having from three to five miles between the ice and the land.

At eight P.M. we neared two other islands, the ice resting on the westernmost, upon which pressure must have been excessive, as large masses were forced nearly over its summit, which was upwards of forty feet.

Between these and the main we ran through a channel in from nine to fifteen fathoms, when an immediate and marked change took place in the general appearance and formation of the land; it became high, precipitous, sterile and rugged, intersected with deep ravines and water courses, having sixty-five fathoms at a quarter of a mile, and fifteen fathoms one hundred yards from the cliffs, which proved exceedingly fortunate, as the whole pack, which had apparently only just broken from the shore, was within half a mile, and in many places so close to it, that, to avoid being beset, we had nearly to touch the land.

Indeed upon several occasions the lower studding sail boom was compelled to be topped up, and poles used to keep the vessel off the grounded ice, which extends all along this coast; nor could we round to, fearful of carrying the jib boom away against its cliffs which here run nearly east and west.

The cape forming its western extreme I have called Prince Alfred in honour of His Royal Highness. [Prince Alfred Cape is on the north-easternmost extremity of Bank's Land.] There were two apparently good harbours about 20 miles to the eastward of the cape; the westernmost had a breakwater half a mile in length, twenty feet high, facing the north, with entrances on its east and west sides sixty yards in breadth; the other was circular, about three-quarters of a mile in diameter, wih its entrance on the west side.

Our critical position would not admit of any detention, otherwise they would have been sounded, being very anxious to find a secure retreat in the event of having to winter on this coast. The weather had been fine, with a S.E. wind, which veered to the W.S.W., bringing fog and rain; so that on the morning of the 20th our farther progress was impeded, by finding the ice resting upon a point which formed a slight indentation of the shore, and was the only place where water could be seen.

To prevent being carried away with the pack, which was filling up its space, we secured to the inshore side of a small but heavy piece of ice, grounded in twelve fathoms, seventy-four yards from the beach; the only protection against the tremendous polar ice (setting a knot per hour to the eastward before a fresh westerly wind), which at 9 P.M. placed us in a very critical position, by a large flow striking the piece we were fast to, and causing it to oscillate so considerably that a tongue, which happened to be under our bottom, lifted the vessel six feet; but by great attention to the anchors and warps, we succeeded in holding on during the conflict, which was continued several minutes, terminating by the floe being rent in pieces, and our being driven nearer the beach. From this until the 29th we lay perfectly secure.

[September 23rd, 1851]

At 3.30 A.M. although not daylight, open water was ascertained to be at hand, from the dark appearence of the horizon to seaward. The vessel was cast off, and standing in that direction we found we were not deceived. The wind during the forenoon coming from the westward, enabled us to run close along the shore, on which still rested a line of thin ice, rendering the entrance of what appeared three good harbours inaccessible . . . At 5.30 P.M. our course was nearly obstructed from the ice resting upon a point about two miles distant; the studding sails were taken in, but almost immediately reset, as it gradually opened allowing just sufficient space for our passage . . .

Miertsching:

[September 23rd, 1851]

At the top of the foremast, as is usual in ice-navigation, a man was stationed named the ice-pilot, who from his lofty post determines the best course of the ship through the ice pieces and communicates this to the officer of the watch on the deck through a long gutta percha trumpet; and the latter directs the ship accordingly. But today none of the men taking turns at this duty could offer any guidance: to repeated questions they invariably answered 'ice everywhere'. So frequently the officer himself would go aloft to ascertain the truth of this 'ice everywhere' – for the ship was going ahead at 5 to 6 knots; but he would find that it was actually so, for the ship was speeding ahead in a short stretch of water beyond which lay impentrable ice as far as one could see. . . .

The seamen had nothing to do: they walked back and forth on the deck, or formed groups discussing this amazing and inexplicable passage . . . interrupted by the roar of the ice-pilot, 'Heavy ice ahead' . . . the sailors flew each to his appointed post to take in sail . . . but before this, a task of two minutes, could be accomplished the ice-pilot cried 'Hold on, the ice is splitting and opening a way for us'. And actually, to the astonishment of all, it was so. Without the least obstruction the ship sailed into this narrow gorge, hemmed in on both sides by lofty walls of ice; on both sides so high that the ends of the ship's yards kept on knocking against it.

M'Clure:

[September 23rd, 1851 – later]

Our course was continued with easy canvas . . . and at 7.30 P.M. with the lead going, went from 15 fathoms up a mud bank while the stern was in five fathoms. The stream anchor and cable were laid out . . . and with clearing the fore-hold and warrant officers' store rooms, and bringing all the weight abaft the mizzen mast, at 10 P.M. we were enabled to heave off, and brought up in six fathoms and a half. The remainder of the night was occupied in restowing the hold, so that by daylight of the 24th we were in perfect readiness to move. On a view of our position we found we were on the N.W. side of a large bay, the eastern limit of which bore N.E. eight miles, which was rapidly filling up with ice flowing in before a fresh gale from the Polar Sea.

I determined to make this our winter quarters; and having remarked on the south side of the bank on which we had grounded a well protected bay, Mr Court was despatched to sound it; and, shortly, making the signal that there was sufficient water, we bore up and at 7.45 A.M. we anchored in four and half fathoms, and that night were firmly frozen in, in what has since proved a most safe and excellent harbour, which, in grateful remembrance of the many perils that we had escaped during the passage of that terrible Polar Sea, we have named the 'Bay of Mercy'.

There the *Investigator* and her crew remained until May 1853, and remarkably all but four officers and men survived the privations of a second and third Arctic winter. In the spring, the crew were able to take a large quantity of game, and the most serious threat to their health, scurvy, was to some extent held in check by the appeerance of large quantities of wild sorrel in the vicinity of Mercy Bay. As Osborn reports: 'All hands that could be spared were daily employed collecting it, – the sick getting the largest share, and the men's messes in turn being next served. Either eaten raw as salad, or cooked, it was extremely palatable, and this was the first succulent vegetable the crew had partaken of since leaving the Sandwich Isles two years before.'

If survival was the first concern of Captain M'Clure and his crew, there were other tasks to be attended to. The most important were the several expeditions by parties under the officers to establish the whereabouts, if any, of other ships in the Arctic regions. Both Cresswell, and 1st Lieutenant Haswell led sledge parties out on these survey trips, and Captain M'Clure with Cresswell took a party along the south coast of Melville Island leaving at Winter Harbour despatches describing the whereabouts of the *Investigator* for anyone coming from the east to find at the Winter Harbour cairn established by Parry thirty-two years earlier.

The survivors of the *Investigator* almost certainly owed their escape to this action, for in 1853, a party *did* reach Winter Harbour, and found the despatches. Even this was not simply by luck, for just such a course was urged on the Admiralty by one of those most closely concerned with the expedition at home, Cresswell's father, Francis.

In an extraordinary episode of unconscious collaboration, Samuel Gurney Cresswell helped lay the trail for his rescuers, and five thousand miles away, his father set those rescuers to look for the clue his son had placed. In March, 1852, when nothing had been heard of the *Investigator* for almost two years, Sir Edward Belcher was preparing a further Arctic expedition, and knowing of this scheme, Francis Cresswell wrote to Augustus Stafford, MP, Secretary of the Admiralty.

Cresswell urged strongly in his letter that the expedition should include in its purposes a search towards Winter Harbour on the south side of Melville Island, and that supplies should be deposited there in case of contact with or need by the crews of the *Investigator* and *Enterprise*. He argued that all the advice given to M'Clure and Collinson (commander of the *Enterprise*) would lead them to seek relief and help along the south shore of Melville Island if their ships could not get through the ice in the vicinity of Bank's Land.

Cresswell's argument was accepted by the Admiralty, in the person of the Duke of Northumberland, First Lord of the

Admiralty, and a paragraph was added to Captain Belcher's instructions to send two ships (the *Resolute* and *Intrepid*) towards Winter Harbour. Without it, *Investigator* and her crew would have been doomed.

When *Resolute* arrived in 1853 off Melville Island a party set out which discovered M'Clure's despatches in Winter Harbour. These gave the whereabouts of the *Investigator* in Mercy Bay, and in consequence a party under Lieutenant Bedford Pim was sent westward to look for the *Investigator*. On 10 March 1853, Lieutenant Pim, accompanied by Dr Domville (both of the *Assistance*) left *Resolute* and *Intrepid* to travel west from their mooring off Melville Island towards Bank's Land where they now knew the *Investigator* to rest. The party travelled for nearly four weeks before, on 6 April 1853, making contact with the stranded sailors.

Captain M'Clure, in the meanwhile, had been preparing two parties of the sickliest members of the crew to try to walk back to civilisation. Thirty men from the crew would be taken by Lieutenants Cresswell and Haswell, leaving something over half the ship's company on board. Cresswell faced the formidable (and probably fatal) task of taking a party of fifteen men westward round Bank's Land to the mouth of the McKenzie river, and so southward to the nearest known depot of the Hudson's Bay company, a journey of a thousand miles.

The other party would try heading eastwards in hope of making contact with whalers who could carry them home. Such plans were very much the last resort, and decided upon only because Captain M'Clure judged these thirty men now too weak to withstand another Arctic winter. The overland journeys, daunting as they were, offered the best chance of survival.

Captain M'Clure was actually discussing these plans, walking a little way from the ship, with Lieutenant Haswell, when they saw a figure approaching across the ice, at first thinking it was a member of their own crew.

'I'm Lieutenant Pim, late of the *Herald,* now in the *Resolute.* Captain Kellett is in her at Dealy Island.' Captain M'Clure was astounded, as his journal records: 'To rush at and seize him by the hand was the first impulse, for the heart was too full for the tongue to speak. The announcement of relief being close at hand, when none was supposed to be even within the Arctic Circle was too sudden, unexpected and joyous for our minds to comprehend it all at once'.

On board ship, the reaction was also almost overwhelming. Cresswell gives this account, in the journal which he kept of his journey from Mercy Bay, to the safety of home exactly six months later:

HMS *Investigator*, Bay of Mercy, April 6th, 1853

The arrival of Lieut. Pim at our ship on the 6th of April was probably the most startling event of my life. We no more expected to see a travelling party at the time than we expected to see the land approaching the ship, or the sun descend from the heavens. The shock was to a degree overpowering to most on board, the men in particular.

I do not pretend to say what other people's might have been, I can merely narrate what I felt and observed myself. It struck me most forcibly that so far from having the effect of elevating it on the contrary had rather the effect of depressing or rather paralysing the mind & faculties. The men might be seen walking about the decks with grave stupified faces.

Several that I spoke to seemed alive to the goodness of an ever masterful providence but at the same time their minds did not appear to be able fully to grasp the extraordinary, almost miraculous change in our circumstances.

This unexpected arrival of course changed all Capt. M'Clure's plans. It was now fixed that I was to take the weakest half of the ships company over to the *Resolute*, leaving our ship on the 15th of April. Capt. M'Clure and Lieut. Pim left the ship on the 8th, between which time and the time of my leaving the ship on the 15th two deaths occured. We thus had to digest the loss of three men within the space of a few days.

My party consisted of the following officers Mr Wynniatt (Mate), Mr Piers (Assistant Surgeon), Mr Miertsching (Esquimaux interpreter) and 24 Petty officers, marines and seamen.

April 15th

Left the ship at 5.30 A.M., the remaining part of the officers and ship's company giving us three hearty cheers. I had one man on the sledge from the time I left the ship until we arrived at the *Resolute*.

The wind blew strong from the Westward with snow drifts, but as I had made all the requisite arrangements for starting I would not postpone it. At 6 A.M. we sighted the Eastern end of the bay, found by it that we had made a good course.

Shortly after leaving the ship, Corporal Farquarson and Joseph Facey broke down and I was obliged to let them fall out from the drag ropes, the former having pains in the chest, the latter suffering from a fall he had shortly before leaving the ship.

4 P.M. Encamped on Point Back about 11 miles from the ship. 6 A.M. Started from Point Back, heavy travelling; 12 noon encamped about five miles from Cape Hamilton.

April 17th

Men much fatigued and many showing signs of weakness, travelling heavy. Encamped after the first trip in the day about ½ a mile from Cape Hamilton, the ice having been thrown up by tremendous external pressures high on the land, between which and the land we had to drag the sledges. To accomplish this I was obliged to double man the sledges, taking two at a time as soon as we found a chance of pushing our way through the hummocky barriers that line this shore.

I struck off onto the sea ice, and encamped about two miles from the land and about half way between Cape Hamilton and the commencement of the cliffs.

April 17th & 18th

The wind prevailing from the Eastward with snow drift and low temperature caused the sick to be very much distressed. We passed over some very heavy old floes on these two days.

April 19th

We had better travelling on this day and made about 10 miles notwithstanding it blowing a gale of wind from the East for part of the day. The fatigue party parted from us at 7 o'clock. I found that many of the men had so far exceeded my orders before leaving the ship that the sledges were much lumbered up with clothing. This is what could not be allowed owing to the weakness of the party, they being barely able to drag themselves and provisions. I therefore gave orders that all the spare clothing should be thrown away or sent back to the ship (by the fatigue party) with the exception of those things that I had directed should be taken before leaving the ship.

The people seemed to think that there was but a very small chance of ever seeing their things again if sent back to the ship, for many of them threw their things away on the floe.

April 20th

Fell in with the Capts' track, but lost it again, the wind having fallen light, and the snow falling.

Cape Hamilton bearing west by south estimated distance 30 miles. Found the travelling to be fair & but little old ice. Made about 10 miles on this day. The ice to the westward of us had much the character of the Polar pack.

12.30 P.M. lost sight of the cliffs of Banks Land. 2 P.M. encamped, people very much fatigued.

April 21st

The weather was so thick that I did not consider it prudent to start before 7 P.M. when we travelled until 10.15 P.M. The weather being so densely thick and there being no wind, I was compelled to trust entirely to the compass.

April 22nd

Weather very thick, travelling fair, passed over a few old floes of no great extent, and much young ice broken up by pressure. Weather continued thick directing our course by compass and casual glimpses of the sun, observed that the ice to the westward of us was heavier than that to the Eastward. Came on Lt. Pim's track and travelled on it for one hour before encamping. Had a glimpse of Melville Island, estimated distance 20 miles, bearing NE.

April 23rd

Melville Island being in sight directed our course for Cape Dundas, travelling sometimes good, sometimes bad, wind Westerly, weather fine.

April 24th

We started at 6.30 A.M. and made very good work for 2½ hours when we got into a pack and shortly after came on several sledge tracks that were probably the tracks of Mr Pim's two sledges on his outward journey. Encamped about five miles from Cape Dundas, from which time until we got close in with the shore about seven miles to the East of Cape Dundas the travelling was very bad, the ice being broken into small fragments and much thrown up by pressure.

On reaching within about four or five hundred yards of the shore the ice became perfectly smooth and the wind having swept it quite clear of snow, it proved the most admirable travelling, and it had not come before it was wanted as my party were in many cases showing signs of weakness.

After travelling for four hours on this fine ice and the wind being fair, going very fast with little or no exertion to the men beyond keeping pace with the sledges I found one of my men to be missing. I was therefore compelled most reluctantly to stop and send a man back for him.

He found the silly fellow about a mile and a half behind in a pool of water that had been caused by the tide flowing up through the cracks inshore. This extraordinary conduct confirmed me in an opinion that I had long held that the man was not sane.

The squalls coming down from the high land under which we were encamped with such tremendous violence that it required the greatest precaution to be taken to prevent the tents being blown down about us.

April 25th & 26th

The weather still continued stormy but as the wind was from the NW it was fair and a great assistance, the ice also continued to be perfectly smooth, a clear indication that there had been open water along this shore in the Autumn.

On the 26th I travelled for 9 hours and was glad to encamp at Cape Providence, the men being much fatigued. Here I found the depot left by Capt. Kellett's parties the previous autumn.

April 27th

We remained camped for 24 hours, many of my party requiring rest. I took 112 lbs of bacon from the cache and left a similar amount of pemmican. This gave the poor fellows quite a treat, and the weather being fine and sun bright, we had a chance of drying all damp things.

The Capt. of my sledge, an old Quartermaster that had been some 30 years at sea informed me that it was a day he should remember to the day of his death.

At 2.50 left Cape Providence. The land after rounding this Cape alters its character very considerably. From Cape Dundas we had been travelling along a continuous line of cliffs which we now lost in low undulating land.

On encamping, five musk oxen were observed on the land about two miles from the tents.

April 28th & 29th

The travelling continued very fair. This was most fortunate as the people were every day showing greater signs of weakness. Many musk oxen were seen during these two days. On the 29th about 15 miles to the westward of Winter Harbour we passed over a very old floe. This was the first old ice we had passed over since leaving.

April 30th

The weather was fine and remarkably warm for the time of year. The people showed many signs of weakness and Charles Anderson was quite unable to walk further. It was therefore a most pleasant consideration that we had but 35 miles further to walk. At 6.30 P.M., just as I was going to make another start, two men were seen coming towards the tents from the eastward. They soon proved to be Mr Pim with a sledge and dogs, he had been sent out by Capt. Kellett to assist us in and land some stores in Winter Harbour. He was much surprised to find us so far advanced in our journey. I wished him to land the things, as we did not require any immediate assistance.

Chas. Anderson being unable to walk, he was taken on the sledge. Notwithstanding this extra weight we made excellent progress, the men being in high spirits on the strength of being so near the *Resolute*.

May 1st

Travelling on Lt. Pim's tracks, sighted the ships.

May 2nd

Started at 11.30 A.M. and arrived on HMS *Resolute* at 4. Capt. Kellett and M'Clure met us on the floe, and Capt. Kellett gave us the most hearty welcome. Little did I think on seeing Capt. Kellett the last person on board the *Investigator* in Bering Straights he would be the first to shake hands with me at Melville Island. We had made the journey from the *Investigator* in 16 days, the distance being 170 miles.

We found the *Resolute* and *Intrepid* nearly deserted, all available strength of both ships away travelling.

Went on shore on Dealy Island, a few Ptarmigan seen. Dined with Capt. Kellett.

May 4th

Dined with the officers of the *Intrepid*. This little ship appeared to be the model of all that is comfortable. Capt. M'Clure left for the *Investigator*, also Dr Domville who was to go across to survey the *Investigator*'s crew. Capt. Kellett much wishes to get up a party of the men to go on to the *North Star*, but as there were but 2 out of the 24 who were not affected with scurvy, it was given up.

May 5th

Capt. Kellett dined in the Gun Room, & Capt Kellett having placed the *Investigator*'s dispatches in my charge for conveyance to England I started with Mr Roche (mate) who was going to travel to the *North Star* with a party of 11 men and the boatswain of the *Resolute*, also with us.

Started with a light sledge and a fair wind. After 3½ days journey found depot that had been left by the *Resolute* in the Autumn. Filled up provisions from it. This increased our weights on the sledge to about a ton and a quarter.

Many herds of Musk oxen were seen on the Island between the point and Dealy Island. We had shot two, and might have shot many more if we had required them.

There had been a good deal of pressure on the eastern end of Melville Island, and we had some difficulty in getting the sledge over the ridges of hummocks; but after getting over these we found the travelling very good and liked it until we got within about 10 miles of Byam Martin Island. We then had some very rough work and sprung one of the uprights of the sledge. On the 13th of May we saw two musk oxen on Point Gilinan. Roche and myself landed to go after them. We wished to have shot only the cow, but having wounded her the bull would not let us approach her we therefore had to shoot him. The sledge being very heavily laden we could not take more than the hinder quarters of the cow away with us, such is Arctic life, or rather such is savage life, for 18 months before leaving the *Investigator* nearly starved and now leaving 8 or 9 hundred pounds of excellent fresh beef for the wolves and foxes.

May 20th

Made the land bearing North, found that in making our course from Byam Martin Island to Cape Cockburn we had made a good deal of southing, the weather had been very thick nearly the whole time.

May 21st

Encamped within about 1½ miles of the shore. A great many bear tracks seen. On the 23rd came upon the Depot left by the *Resolute* about 10 miles to the Eastward of Cape Cockburn. Found that the bears had broken open a box of preserved meat and gnawed through several of the tins. Our journey now continued with but little to vary it with the exception of shooting a bear, until the 26th when Mr Roche and myself went on shore on Baker Island where many deer were seen and one shot. We might have shot more, but had not ammunition. I was quite surprised to see deer here as not any of Capt. Austin's parties had seen any when near McDougal Bay.

There was every reason for believing that the large game such as musk oxen and deer were very plentiful on the Southern shores of the Parry Islands during the spring. Called at Assistance Harbour and visited the Depot. This is a tolerably good harbour but I do not consider it to be much protected from a southerly gale. At the time of our passing there was much hummocky ice in it and it had evidently been thrown up by pressure.

Visited depot and boat at Cape Hotham and on the morning of the 2nd arrived on board HMS *North Star*.

June 2nd

The *North Star* had been driven on shore by the ice in a gale of wind on the 28th of September. The severe weather then setting in and there being much heavy ice round her, it was found to be impracticable to get her off. She therefore remained on the ground all the winter. I went on shore to see the graves and other traces of this place having been Franklin's winter quarters.

June 3rd

Mr Alsten (Mate) left the ship with one man and four dogs for his return to the *Resolute*. It was probable that he would reach his destination in 12 or 14 days. Had a strong gale from the SE.

June 5th

Snow and thick weather.

June 7th

A wolf was seen today. This is the first one that has been seen at Beechey Island.

Friday June 10th

Walked down to Caswell's tower; two geese seen on the low land.

June 18th

A boarding pike with a hand painted on a piece of wood and nailed to the top of it was picked up on this day by the master. It was found on the plain going to Caswell's and had evidently been a direction post, but as it had fallen down, there is no saying in which direction it had pointed.

June 25th

Made all sail on the ship and hove on the purchases without any effect.

June 26th

Succeeded in moving the ship 42 feet ahead.

June 27th

Hove the ship 21 feet ahead at high water.

June 28th

Moved the ship 28 feet.

July 1st

Employed watering ship, getting cables on board and preparing for sea.

July 4th

A shooting party went away and encamped on the plain.

July 5th

Walked to Caswell's Tower, found a bottle with a few shot in it. Much water running off the land, some of the streams so deep and rapid that it was with the greatest difficulty I got across. Shot a red throated diver, King Duck, 2 Arctic gulls &c.

July 6th

A bear seen from the ship. Passed top gallant yards. Completed water. A shooting party sent away. The previous one had been most unfortunate only having shot two or three ducks.

July 8th

Preparing equipment for a boat and sledge party.

July 11th

Capt. Pullen left the ship with a party of one officer and ten men and boat and sledge for the purpose of communicating with or conveying despatches within reach of Sir Edward Belcher.

July 17th

Employed getting ballast on board.

July 20th

Capt. Pullen having expressed a wish that I should attend to the fitting of the *Mary* Yacht (as it was not improbable that I might have to go down to the whalers, or possibly home in her). I went on board and found that she wanted all sorts of repairs. The carpenters were set to work on her at once.

July 21st

The crack across the mouth of the harbour opened to the breadth of about 30 yards.

July 23rd

Crack opened to 60 yards, no other change in the state of the ice.

Friday July 28th

Observed a wide opening in the ice off the harbour mouth.

July 30th

Open water seen.

August 1st

Ice in the offing in motion. Several hares seen, four or five shot. Two casks with notices in were put in the open water.

August 3rd

The ice in Barrow Strait slowly drifting to the Eastward.

August 4th

Much open water seen from the Island.

August 5th

Employed on board in heaving down the canal and floating the ice past the ship.

August 6th

A broad lane of water seen extending towards Cape Hotham from Cape Spencer.

August 8th

We had every reason to expect a ship out from England, but the breaking up of the ice having been so so very late, none of us expected her at Beechey Island before the 20th. It was therefore a most agreeable surprise to see a large steamer [HMS *Phoenix*] with a transport in tow rounding Cape Riley.

Went on board to pay my respects to Captain Inglefield, and received letters up to May.

The *Phoenix* went down to Cape Riley and commenced landing coals by means of a derrick rigged on the cliff. Capt. Inglefield started in a gig to go up Wellington Channel on the 10th.

August 11th

Captain Pullen returned having communicated with Sir Ed. Belcher who was at sea. All well on board his ships. He wintered in harbour in nearly the position of Sir J. Franklin as laid down by Parry. His parties had communicated with Capt. Kellett and had also discovered that Jones Sound communicated with Wellington Channel. There had been much open water where he was in May, but the navigable polar basin, animal life and higher temperature have all proved to be humbug.

August 12th

The French lieutenant of the *Phoenix*, M. Bellot left the ship to try and communicate with Sir Edward Belcher.

August 17th

Capt. Inglefield came on board the *North Star* to hold a survey on invalids. It blew a tremendous gale during the night. I do not remember having ever seen so tremendous a gale in the Arctic regions. We broke adrift and drove some way back up the canal. We all felt very anxious about the ships on the floe edge, but had our anxiety relieved by their making the signal at daylight that they were all right.

I walked down to the *Phoenix* with Capt. Inglefield. I never saw a more extraordinary scene than the ice to seaward presented. I have seen much heavier ice thrown up by pressure, but never have seen ice so thoroughly ground up and pounded by the violence of natural pressure. Many of the ridges were 12 or 14 feet above the sea, I do not know that any written description would offer any adequate idea of this. The only thing I can compare it to is all the stone masons' yards in the world being tumbled and jumbled together. Amongst this wild chaos was the poor *Phoenix*.

It was with some difficulty we got on board, clumbering and climbing over the ridges, mounds, hummocks, points, and angles of ice that intervened between the land, floe and ship, a distance of about 80 yards. After a proper quantity of tumbling down and getting up again, slipping with one leg in the water, and then the other, we contrived to get on board, and found that they had a dreadful night of it. The ship had been lifted several feet by pressure, and complained much, but it was believed that no damage had been done.

Returned to the *North Star*.

Saturday August 20th

Two of the men that had started with Lt. Bellot returned with the disturbing intelligence that M. Bellot had been drowned. They gave the following account of the sad event.

The ice they were travelling on was broken up by the gale on Wednesday night. They endeavoured to reach the land by Halketts* boat that they had with them, and had got all their provisions and tent gear on shore, and the boat was being rowed to M. Bellot and the two men remaining on the ice, when the ice commenced drifting rapidly from off the land. The men on shore waited until they lost sight of those on the ice, and then commenced their return to the ship. They stopped some time at Cape Bowden to rest when to their great surprise the two men that had been drifted off the land on the ice rejoined them. They had drifted back to the land after the gale almost by a miracle, and got on shore. They had been on the ice for nearly two days.

It appears that Lt. Bellot had built a snow house for the men and had been in it some time when he went out to look round to see if he could make out the land. His long absence from them caused the men to go out to look for him but found nothing but his stick, and as the floe was not of great extent it is impossible to help coming to the painful conclusion that he must have been blown from the ice and drowned. Thus perished as brave and nobly distinguished fellow as ever lived.

Joined the *Phoenix* for a passage to England.

August 21st

The ice setting fast to the Westward and closing on the land floe, we cast off from Cape Riley and made fast to the land floe a little to the westward of the cape. The ship in swinging round touched the ground abaft. This was in the first watch. In the middle watch the ship was beset and drifted to the westward. At 2.40 A.M. the ice having opened to the eastward we took *Breadalbane* in tow and proceeded to the Eastward amongst heavy floes and packed ice. At 3.20, not being able to get any nearer Cape Riley, the ice having closed, made fast to land floe. *Breadalbane* one cable's length from us outside, drifting to the westward. Shortly after 4 a very heavy nip came on the ship and the hands were turned up to desert the ship should it be necessary.

The *Breadalbane* was not so strong as the *Phoenix*, or the pressure was heavier on her, for she was stove by the ice, and sank within 15 minutes.

The weather during the night had been fine and calm. After church commenced cutting a dock, but the ice opening went down to Cape Riley and made fast in our old position.

---

* Folding portable boat.

Later, safe at home, Cresswell gave a detailed account of the loss of the *Breadalbane*:

About twelve or one o'clock I heard a great pressure of ice coming on the ship. We were at that time made fast to the land ice about a mile off the land; the ship was alongside of the ice.

The floe, or sea ice, which might be 20 or 30 miles in extent was closing in upon the land ice, and unless the ship was protected in some way, the probability was that it would crush her. I was asleep in my cabin at the time, when the first Lieutenant came down and said the captain had ordered all hands to turn out to be in readiness to desert the ship. I heard the ship's timber creaking and groaning, and making a most unpleasant noise; but we had experienced a great deal of noise in the *Investigator*, and I had thought nothing of it.

I jumped on deck and then saw the ice had passed us and was going on to the *Breadalbane*. It took the *Breadalbane* and nipped her. It is generally considered that if a ship is nipped and she rises, the ice getting under her, she is safe; but if she does not rise, then it is very probable she will be destroyed. In this case the ship rose. I thought therefore nothing more about it and went down to my bed again. The *Breadalbane* was only about 300 yards from us.

About 10 minutes after that an officer came down and said 'If you want to see the last of the *Breadalbane*, you must get on deck.' I jumped up and went on deck, but there was not a vestige of her to be seen, the men had jumped on the ice. This is just the way the ship was destroyed by the ice.*

August 22nd

The ice in places having opened, and it being broken by the late gale we made the best of our way towards the *North Star*, and reached within about ½ a mile of her. The rudder having been much crushed by the ice, lifted it. The screw had also received considerable injury, this was also lifted.

---

* The loss of the *Breadalbane* as recounted after Cresswell's return to King's Lynn, October, 1853.

August 23rd

The ice had gone off from the land so very rapidly that not any was to be seen from the deck. This was caused by the NW wind. Employed discharging stores, the *North Star*'s dingy was crushed alongside.

August 24th

Lighted fires and got the steam up. Proceeded out of the bay, much heavy ice seen to the Southward of us.

August 25th

At 3 A.M. Came to a dead block; made fast to a heavy piece of grounded ice. In the afternoon we again made a start, weather very thick, but did not proceed far before we were again stopped by the ice. We most fortunately got into a snug little harbour that Mr Manson, Ice Master, had discovered when on shore in the morning and anchored. (The harbour has been named Graham Harbour in compliment to the 1st Lord of the Admiralty.) Before midnight it blew hard from the eastward.

August 26th

Blowing a heavy gale from the Eastward, several hares shot, ship hove, but she fortunately brought up on the 2nd anchor being let go before we had drifted on the lee ice.

Sunday August 28th

Found one of the lower deck beams sprung, supposed it to have been done off Beachey Island. Lost starboard anchor in trying to weigh it (it being under the ice). At 9 o'clock got under weigh and went out of the harbour, but the ice master did not consider it prudent to proceed as the ice was close and the night dark, returned and anchored.

Sept 1st

The ice having drifted off shore considerably during the night got steam up and proceeded to the Eastward (at 4.30. AM). Had to pass through a good deal of heavy ice, the ice of the Capes almost always being close in shore. At 1 made fast to the land ice at 6 cast off from it and proceeded. Very squally weather from the NW.

Sept 2nd

Communicated with the natives of Dundas Harbour.

Sept 3rd

Cleared Lancaster sound. Last sight of land.

Sept 4th

Fine fair wind Studding sails set. Flocks of loons flying to the Southward Lat 75°20'N Long 70°30'W.

Sept 5th

Fine fair wind during the greater part of the day.

Sept 6th

Sounded with 2870 fathoms of line, no bottom Lat 73°3', Long 64°56'. Got the steam up, the wind being light.

Sept 7th

Passed through much heavy ice during the night. In the morning the wind being fair stopped the engines and made all sail.

Sept 8th

At 7.30 land was observed on the port bow and shortly after Disco was in sight. At 3.40 shortened sail and altered course for the Wright channel. Made and shortened sail as requisite. Running through the Wright Channel in the first watch, it being very dark we nearly ran into an iceberg. The ship was going at the time at about six knots. The berg was just seen in time to stop and give her a back turn. If we had been 10 seconds later in seeing the berg and reversing the engines we should have been right into it. The consequence would have been that we should have gone down like a stone.

Sept 9th

An immense number of ducks seen 7.30. Pilot came on board, steamed into LPevely harbour.

Lievely harbour is a very snug little place and sheltered from all winds. I believe it is the best harbour in Greenland.

Sept 10th

Commenced coaling. Went on shore to call on the Inspector and Governor. Went on shore in the evening and had a dance with the belles of Lievely. One family, the Biobaggr family by name were decidedly good looking and very clean. The girls danced with spirit *and without any affectation*, they also sang many songs. It is wonderful their ear for music. There was dancing every night that we remained here. I asked one of the girls if she was not tired. Her answer was that she could dance all night for every night in the week without being tired.

Sept 14th

It blew a heavy gale and caused us to strike the Top Gallant Mast and yards. Burned rockets and blue lights to amuse the Natives.

Sept 15th

The Danish Inspector and Governor came on board to dine with the Gun Room officers and we had a very jolly evening of it and wound up with a dance on shore.

Sept 16th

Preparing for sea.

Sept 17th

Five A.M. Shortened in cable. 5.40, weighed and steamed out of Lievely.

Sept 18th

Arrived at Holsteinborg, anchored at 2.40 in the afternoon. Found at anchor here whaler *True Love*, Mr Parker master. He had been caught in a most violent gale on the 14th. It blew all his sails out of the bolt ropes, and the ship striking a heavy piece of ice stove her port bow in. Fortunately for him the wind enabled him to shape a course for Holsteinborg keeping on the port tack which kept the hole in his bows out of water. He had caught 9 fish; this gives about 100 tons of oil. The Governor and deputy came on board, then we went on shore.

Sept 19th

Went on shore shooting. Did not see anything in the way of game, walking very troublesome from the heavy fall of snow during the night. Went on shore and had a dance.

Sept 20th

5.30 weighed. Took *True Love* in tow and proceeded out of the harbour. In making Holsteinborg Mount Cunningham is the best guide,

Above: Watercolour sketch by Cresswell of the English Channel made in 1834, when he was seven years old. His skill as a young artist is equalled by his attention to the detail of the rigging and gear of the boats, including sailing and steam ships.

Left: Cresswell in the Naval uniform of a volunteer, painted in 1842 just as he set out in HMS *Agincourt* for a five-year voyage. He was fourteen and a half, and had twenty years in the Navy ahead of him.
By B. DelaCour.

Above: HMS *Agincourt* in harbour at Hong Kong. Admiral Sir Thomas Cochrane's flagship was based at Hong Kong from autumn 1842 until December, 1846. The settlement was already a bustling port, and here a junk-rigged sampan passes *Agincourt* towards the town.

Below: HMS *Agincourt* under sail. On 3 January 1844 Cresswell writes: 'We have been a cruise to sea ... to try rate of sailing', Admiral Cochrane's *Agincourt versus* Admiral Sir William Parker's *Cornwallis*, seen to shoreward here. 'The next day we decidedly licked her'.

HMS *Investigator* and HMS *Enterprise* at Whale Fish Islands, June-July 1848. 'This is the queerest place I was ever in, nothing but a lot of small rocky barren islands', but with a great many birds the ship's crews shot for the table.

Esquimaux before their settlement at Whale Fish Islands, 'not a bit of vegetation except in one spot where the Esquimaux huts are', Cresswell noted on June 29th, 1848.

Esquimaux woman. 'I cannot say I am agreeably surprised with the Esquimaux ... filthy, dirty, oily, dreadfully ugly ... The women are a shade better than the men'. But they were skilled people, 'it is very wonderful the way they throw the spear'.

Investigator and *Enterprise* under sail off Greenland. In the background the 'Devil's Thumb' rock, a natural feature which occurs in several of Cresswell's views of the Greenland coast. 'I have taken great pains with my drawing since I have been away', he wrote home.

Enterprise and *Investigator* under sail off Greenland. Beyond the ships, the Devil's Thumb is prominent. This cruise in search of Sir John Franklin in 1848-9 ended when thick ice from the previous hard winter blocked the further progress of the two ships.

Travelling party encampment. The men of the Arctic exploration ships spent much time away from the ships. Sir James Ross took a party in a fruitless search for traces of Sir John Franklin in 1848-9, and Cresswell himself led a party home in 1853.

Left: *Investigator* and *Enterprise* in Glacier Bay, July 1848. The glacier is prominent on the left. In the foreground the dinghy suggests men out for a recreational row, but with a shotgun aboard to the big bags of game which Cresswell reports as taken by both ships.

Below: Cutting into Port Leopold, 1848. The ice has formed on open water, and is less rough than old or tumbled pack ice. The ship's crew manoeuvre the vessel towards a sheltered spot in the bay where the ships were to spend the winter.

Opposite top: Winter quarters, 1848. *Investigator* and *Enterprise* under awnings and snow-cover in the Arctic sun. 'This is a very snug place, and as we can't get any further to the north... we must make ourselves very jolly here' Cresswell wrote from Port Leopold.

Opposite below: *Investigator* in sight of Banks' Land, September 6, 1850. Capt. M'Clure wrote: 'At 11.30 AM, high land was observed on the port bow ...' when ashore, 'we observed numerous traces of reindeer, hare, and wild fowl; moss and divers species of flowers'.

Lord Nelson's Head. Capt. M'Clure writes: 'By 9.30 of the 7th of September we were off the South Cape, a fine bold headland, the cliffs rising perpendicularly upwards of a thousand feet, which was named "Lord Nelson's Head" in memory of the hero connected with Arctic adventure'.

Moonlit seascape. The profile of Banks' Land shows the same rugged outline as Nelson's Head. Cresswell is here using the imaginative technique of distancing himself from the ship to capture the scene. *Investigator* is alone as *Enterprise* has been left behind.

Investigator at Princess Royal Island, September 10, 1850. The mixture of open water and drifting pack ice and small bergs was the more benign of conditions in the Arctic sea. *Investigator* was to encounter much more severe weather in the neighbourhood of Banks' Land.

Sledge travelling party, Bank's Land, 1851. Many parties were sent out from *Investigator*. Cresswell went on several, the most crucial being that which left notice of her position (in 1853) to be found at Winter Harbour on Melville Island by her eventual rescuers.

In the pack, 1851. Here crew members are securing HMS *Investigator* against drifting ice by using anchors and warps to prevent the vessel being carried away or damaged. A more dramatic occasion of this sort was recorded by Cresswell on 20 August 1851.

23 September 1851. *Investigator* running north-east of Banks Land. Miertsching writes: 'The ship sailed into this narrow gorge, hemmed in on both sides by the lofty walls of ice, on both sides so high that the ship's yards kept on knocking against it.'

The dramatic position of *Investigator* during her first winter in the Arctic. M'Clure writes: 'On the 8th of October our perplexities terminated with a nip that lifted the vessel a foot, and heeled her 30 degrees to port, in which position we quietly remained'.

Melville Island from Bank's Land. Though *Investigator* never reached Melville Island, sledge parties did, and completed on foot the North-West Passage that lies to the right of this view. This sketch is drawn from high ground close to Bay of Mercy where *Investigator* was moored.

Above: Bay of Mercy. On 15 April 1853, Lt. Cresswell set out with his sledge party of the weakest crew members from *Investigator*. The start of a long journey home, the first stage took 16 days to cover 170 miles to HMS *Resolute*.

Below: 17 April 1853 near Cape Hamilton: Cresswell writes: 'The ice having been thrown up by tremendous external pressures ... I was obliged to double man the sledges ... taking two at a time ... pushing our way through the hummocky barriers that line this shore'.

Above: Civic Reception, King's Lynn, October 28th, 1853. Celebrating Cresswell's safe return, Sir Edward Parry said: 'You have before you about the oldest and the youngest of Arctic navigators ... I came 200 miles, and would have been glad to come 2,000 this day'.

Below: Grand Naval Review, Spithead, April 1856. Cresswell wrote: 'It was more a wonderful than a beautiful sight. Fancy a large manufacturing town under weigh'. This was because the ships were under steam, not sail, as they passed under their Sovereign's Review.

Above: Sailing at Cowes. In summer 1856 Cresswell cruised the Solent in HMS *Sparrowhawk*, and frequently comments on the high winds and rain. Here three sloops tackle rough water with *Sparrowhawk* or a sister steam and sail despatch vessel in the background.

Below: Up river, Ning Po, April 1858. Scene at the head of the navigable stretch of the river, up which Cresswell and his party took a holiday excursion. 'My boat was about 30 feet long, 6 broad with a cabin covered in about 12 feet long'.

Above: Encounter in the South Atlantic. *Surprise* meeting a troopship bound for the Indian Mutiny. Cresswell writes: 'We found as she got near us she was full of troops, and a lot of ladies and officers on the poop. They manned the rigging and cheered us'.

Below: Rafting in China, 1858. Cresswell and friends visited a temple in the hills behind Ning Po. After several days walking and pick-nicking, 'The homeward journey we did by foot and raft. The river is navigated by bamboo rafts, it being much to shallow for boats'.

Attack on pirate junks at Ling Ting, near Hong Kong, 1858. HMS *Surprise* provides covering fire for the boats of HMS *Cambrian*, under the command of Lt. J W Webb. Twenty-six pirate junks were taken or destroyed, and Cresswell was promoted Captain for his part.

A pirate junk blows up during the assault by *Surprise* at Ling Ting. In Cresswell's account the detonation of this junk ended the resistance by the pirates, who deserted their junks and fled. During this battle, Cresswell seized 327 guns mounted by the pirates.

the peak on the top of it being very remarkable. 4.30 P.M. cast off the *True Love*, Lat 66°27'N, Long 54°00'W.

Sept 21st

Up and down steam as the wind favoured or not. Lat. at noon 64°2'N, Long 55°6'W.

Sept 22nd

Lat. 61°22'N, Long. 54°48'W Weather very squally.

Sept 23rd

Wind variable. Made and shortened sail as requisite. Made good since yesterday 183 miles.

Sept 24th

At noon Lat 58°18'N Long 47°54'W. Butt of Lewis N. 89, E 1,268 miles. Ship rolling very heavily. Aurora seen brilliantly.

Sept 25th

Latitude 58°6'N Longitude 44°1'W. Butt of Lewis N 88, E 1,152 miles.

———————————

Ten days after this entry on HMS *Phoenix*, Cresswell was safely home from his epic voyage.

———————————

HMS *Phoenix*, October 4, 1853

Dearest Parents,

God has heard your prayers and has returned me to you safe and well.

I write this on board the *Phoenix* in which ship I am taking a passage to England having left our ship the *Investigator* on the 15th of last April. She was wintering in Banks Land about 60 miles from Melville Island.

Capt. Kellett's travelling party found our ship on the 6th April. They had been guided to our whereabouts by a notice we left at Winter Harbour, Melville Island.

I have had letters from you up to May of this year, and I also got one on the 6th of April, one that you sent to Capt. Kellett. I cannot express the relief that they were to me. We are now about 60 miles from Cape Wrath (Scotland), and as we are going about 8 knots shall be through the Pentland Firth tomorrow. Capt. Inglefield and myself will land probably at Aberdeen. I write this so as to be able to send it by the very first chance.

Ten thousand congratulations to Frank and best love to my dear Sister whom I long to see.

> Ever your most affect. Son,
> S.G.Cresswell.

H.M.S. *Phoenix* at sea.

P.S. In haste, railway train 60 miles from Town, Oct 6th, 4 A.M., do not come to Town as I shall probably be at Lynn tomorrow. I put up at the Ship Inn, Charing Cross.

Within days, Cresswell was back at Lynn, where the joy at the local hero's return was not confined to his family. Within the month a Civic Reception had been organised and an Address composed to be presented to the young man at dinner held in the city's Guild Hall.

Among the guests was Admiral Sir Edward Parry, Cresswell's friend, sponsor and predecessor in the Arctic ice. The Reception gave both Cresswell and Parry the pleasing chance to discuss each other's feats, and compare notes before a gratifyingly excited audience.

On 26 October, after receiving his handsomely engrossed Address from the Borough of Lynn, Cresswell gave the following account of his voyage, to be responded to by Parry:

For the last three centuries it has been the great endeavour of England to try and discover a shorter route to India by the North-West Passage, that is by forcing a passage from the Atlantic, through Baffin's bay, and round the north of America, through Bering's straights to India, and that from the time of Henry VIII expeditions have been continually going from England, but have always failed . . . Sir Edward Parry's discoveries are most wonderful (cheers). He entered from Lancaster Sound, which had never been discovered before, and proceeded in the ships for 900 miles to the westward, where ship had never been before, and arrived at Melville Island; from whence to the extreme point reached by the *Investigator* is only a distance of between 60 and 70 miles. So that the North-West Passage has been discovered, or rather gone over by the ships with that exception, and travelling parties have gone over the rest of it.

We sailed in Jan. 1850, and after going round America and passing the straights of Magellan and touching at the Sandwich Isles, we met the ice to the west of Point Barrow. We made our way along this coast with great difficulty, till we got off the mouth of the Mackenzie . . . Our autumn travelling parties established the fact of there being a North-West Passage, which it fell to our fortune to discover on 26th October (this very day) in 1850.

In the following year, the summer of 1851 our great object was to push through so as to carry our ship home through the North-West Passage. We got some distance and then found the ice so excessively heavy from the north and eastward that we were obliged to put back.

In September 1851 it came on to blow a most violent gale off the land. It blew for three days, and on the fourth the ice opened up a little, and after considerable dangers and difficulties we succeeded in getting into Mercy Bay where we wintered the last two winters, 1851-2 and 1852-3. In the spring of this year 1853 it became absolutely necessary that some of us should leave the ship to save the others from starving . . .

I was accordingly ordered by Capt M'Clure to abandon the ship, and I went with half the ship's company and travelled over the ice to Capt. Kellet. It was about 170 miles. Perhaps you would like to hear something about our daily arrangements for travelling, as Arctic travelling is rather a novelty.

You must be aware that in Arctic travelling you must depend entirely on your own resources. You will not have a single thing to depend on, no produce of the country, or firewood or coals, or anything of the sort; and whatever you have to take to sustain you for the journey you must carry or drag.

It is found by experience more easy to drag it on sledges than to carry it. The plan we adopt is this: we have a sledge generally manned by about six or ten men. We load this with provisions, with tents, and all requisites for travelling; simple cooking utensils, spirits of wine for cooking &c.

&c., and start off. The quantity people can generally drag is about 40 days' provisions; that gives about 200lbs weight to each.

After starting from the ship, and travelling on from a certain number of hours – generally about 10 or 11 – we then encamp for the night, or rather for the day, because it is considered best to travel at night and sleep in the day, on account of the glare of the sun on the snow.

We used to travel all night, about 10 hours, and then encamp, light our spirits of wine, put our small kettle on it to thaw the snow water and after we had our supper – just a piece of pemmican and a glass of water, we were very glad to get in after smoking our pipes ('Bravo' and laughter). The first thing we did after pitching our tent was to lay a sort of mackintosh cloth over the snow. On this would be a piece of buffalo robe stretched. Each man and officer had a blanket sewed up in the form of a bag, and this we used to jump into, much the same as you may see a boy in a sack (laughter). We lay down head and feet, the next person having his feet to my head, and his head to my feet, just the same as herrings in a barrel (laughter). After this we covered ourselves with skins over the whole of us, and the closer we got the better, as there was more warmth (laughter). We lay till morning, and then the process was the same again.

Capt. Kellett wished to send our men on to Beechey Island where there was another ship stationed, but they were too unwell to go for 22 out of the 24 men I brought out with me had the scurvy. Therefore I volunteered, as I had good health myself, to go on and take a chance of any ship that might come out there, as it was very important that information should be conveyed to England as soon as possible, apprising the Admiralty of the safety of the *Investigator* because otherwise there was no saying what expeditions might have been put forth and what lives might have been perilled in looking for us . . . Ladies and gentlemen I shall not detain you any longer, as I am afraid I have detained you too long already.

In reply, Sir Edward Parry said:

It is now 28 years since I had the honour of receiving within these walls the freedom of the ancient borough of Lynn. I can truly say that from that moment to this I have never witnessed any occasion which has given me more high delight and gratification than this. You have before you today about the oldest and the youngest of Arctic navigators. And I do assure you fom my heart that the feelings of the old Arctic navigator are of the very highest and most intense gratification he ever experienced in the whole course of his life.

I rejoice to be here to meet and support my dear young friend as my fellow townsman. I may call him my fellow townsman, being a freeman myself of your borough. I feel therefore the greatest delight and gratification in being able to come here. I came 200 miles, and would willingly have come 2,000 to be present this day . . . It is a matter of great and earnest thankfullness to Almighty God to have been permitted to receive back our dear gallant young friend.

I have been delighted with the plain simple intelligent, and I must say modest, account he has given of himself. Nothing can be more complete and perfect than the summary he has given you, in so short a time, of the Arctic discovery. How little I thought when I stood upon the western part of Melville Island, and discovered Bank's Land in the distance (we called it 60 miles), that from the cape which I named after many difficulties, Cape Providence – that there would in the course of time come a ship the other way to meet me and to be anchored in the Bay of Mercy. I admire the feeling which induced Capt. M'Clure and his companions to give that name to the place which had harboured them under circumstances of such extreme peril (loud applause).

The banquet at Lynn marked the close of Cresswell's most significant adventure, securing for him (and Lt Wynniatt) the unique place as the first men ever to travel entirely round the American continent. However, there are two footnotes to the story. At first it looked as though Cresswell would continue in the Arctic service, when the following appeared in *The Morning Chronicle*:

February 23rd, 1854
London: Captain Edward Augustus Inglefield (1853), who made two previous voyages to the Arctic regions . . . bringing home Lieutenant

Cresswell of the *Investigator*, the first European who accomplished the North-West Passage, having entered through Bering's Straits and returned to England by Davis' Straits, is appointed to command the *Phoenix*, screw steam-sloop, Woolwich, commissioned yesterday for the purpose of conveying further relief, during the approaching season, for Sir Edward Belcher's expedition . . .

Lt Samuel Gurney Cresswell (1849) who has been on the books of the *Investigator*, which he left last year in Mercy Bay in the Arctic regions on his return to England with despatches from Captain M'Clure, is appointed to be lieutenant-commander of the *Talbot*, 22, commissioned yesterday at Deptford, to convey stores to Beechey Island, and to accompany the *Phoenix* in her next voyage to the Arctic regions.

Cresswell did not accept the appointment to the *Talbot* under Inglefield's command, and within a week, *The Morning Herald* used his appointment to HMS *Archer* to explain why not:

March 2nd, 1854

London: In the list of appointments last night we find that of Lt. S.G. Cresswell, to the *Archer*, 14, screw, Woolwich. We therefore presume that Mr Cresswell has declined the appointment of Lieutenant Commander under Captain Inglefield, and the whole Naval service will applaud Lieut. Cresswell for his spirit. As an officer and a gentleman it would be most distasteful for Lieut. Cresswell to serve as a lieutenant under the officer who was promoted for bringing home those despatches of which he, Lieut. Cresswell was the bearer; he (Lt Cresswell) having been the officer who actually made the North-West Passage under Captain M'Clure.

The whole affair is most discreditable to the Admiralty; and although a lieutenant, Mr Cresswell stands higher in the estimation of the service and the public than either the Board of Admiralty who have neglected him, or the officer who has come between him and his just reward for unprecedented services.

Meanwhile, Cresswell had not been idle. Between his arrival back in October and the following spring, he had been at work with his brushes. The result was a set of eight water-colour sketches (as he always called them) of the adventures of HMS *Investigator* in the Arctic.

These pictures are studio versions of the sketches he made at sea and on the ice. Once the eight pictures were completed, lithographs were commissioned for publication and sale. The colour lithographs have been exhibited at, for instance, the National Maritime Museum on the occasion of an exhibition about Franklin, and are well known both to naval historians, and to descendants of Cresswell's family and friends.

Cresswell hoped their success might help him in his naval career, and at least, as *The Times* reported, they were the occasion for a Royal audience for the 27-year-old Lieutenant at Buckingham Palace:

March 22nd, 1854

London: Lieutenant Gurney Cresswell.

The Queen having been pleased to command Lieutenant Samuel Gurney Cresswell, formerly of the *Investigator* discovery ship, and the first to accomplish the North-West Passage, to attend at Buckingham Palace, the enterprising young officer had the honour of complying with her Majesty's commands on Monday, and submitted his sketches made by him during his service in the *Investigator*, and exhibiting some of the most interesting scenes brought under his notice during the discovery of the North-West Passage by Captain M'Clure. Her Majesty examined the drawings minutely, and put numerous questions to Lieutenant Cresswell relative to the long and hazardous voyage of the *Investigator* which he answered to the entire satisfaction of the Queen. The Sketches are to be, by special permission, dedicated to Her Majesty.

This episode was the most intimate contact Cresswell had with his Sovereign; not many of Victoria's sailors would have found themselves discussing ice-floes, and no doubt polar bears and sledges with the Queen, and what is more when aged only twenty-six. Cresswell was to encounter the Queen both at

Court *levees* and as an escort to the Royal Yacht in later years, but these formal occasions and exercises can hardly have compared with chatting to the Queen over the equivalent of today's travel snaps, however exceptional their provenance, and significant the discovery of the North-West Passage they recorded.

Appendix

In his *The Discovery of the North West Passage*, Sherard Osborn publishes two tables illustrating graphically the circumstances of Arctic life. The first charts the maximum and minimum temperatures experienced by the Investigator's crew 1850-53. For the sake of brevity, these are given quarterly:

Degrees Farenheit. Freezing is + 32 degrees.

	Maximum	Minimum	Mean (degrees of frost)
1850: IVth quarter	+24	-40	-11 (-43)
1851: I	-5	-51	-33 (-65)
II	+53	-32	+17 (-15)
III	+52	+1	+33 (+1)
IV	+26	-44	-7 (-39)
1852: I	+8	-52	-27 (-59)
II	+51	-38	+40 (+8)
III	+52	-4	+30 (-2)
IV	+16	-48	-16 (-48)
1853: I	-16	-65	-34 (-66)

(Quarterly figures based on daily and monthly data)

Osborn's other revealing table shows the tally of game meat taken by the crew of the *Investigator* while in the Arctic, showing that the tinned and dried rations they took with them were supplemented by fresh meat, taken by their own hand (and firearms).

Game Taken, 1850–53

	Number	Average Weight (lbs)	Total Weight (lbs)
Musk Oxen	7	278	1,945
Deer	110	70lbs	7,716
Hares	169	6lbs	1,014
Grouse	186	Not weighed	–
Duck	198	” ”	–
Geese	29	” ”	–
Wolves	2	” ”	–
Bears	4	” ”	–

Total head of game killed: 1,005.

THREE

HMS *Archer, April-December 1854*

Even before Cresswell had received his Audience with Queen Victoria, the scene was being prepared for his next service in the Crimean War. Relations with Russia had been deteriorating fast before the dispatch of a fleet to the Crimea, and the French and British had determined that a fleet must also be sent to the north Russian coast in the Baltic sea. Cresswell volunteered for the Baltic fleet.

The initial British fleet under the command of Vice-Admiral Sir Charles Napier comprised fifteen vessels, from HMS *Duke of Wellington*, flagship, 131 guns, to HMS *Dragon*, paddle vessel, 6 guns. This fleet sailed from Spithead on 11 March 1854, and made its Baltic headquarters at Kioge Bay, on the Danish coast south of Copenhagen.

The fleet of fifteen vessels marked an important moment in naval history, being the first time an exclusively steam-powered fleet set out to war from Britain. Later the squadron was joined by sailing as well as steam vessels, to form a mixed force.

From Kioge Bay the fleet was to patrol east and northwards as far as Cronstadt, at the eastern end of the Gulf of Finland, on Russia's northwest coast. The objects of the fleet included blockading the Russian Baltic ports, and protecting Danish and Swedish territory from attack by Russia. The urgency in despatching a fleet to the Baltic even before war had been declared was emphasised by the size of the Russian fleet in the Gulf of Finland.

Other ships were being prepared for the Baltic campaign, and on 2 March Cresswell was appointed as Lieutenant in HMS *Archer*, 13-gun corvette. He was to serve on board *Archer* until December when the Russian ports in the Baltic became frozen in and the blockading fleet was able to withdraw.

During the fitting-out of the *Archer*, and the voyage out, the urgency of the situation increased, with Anglo-Russian relations deteriorating further. War was officially declared while *Archer* was at sea, and on 4 April, by which time *Archer* had arrived in Denmark, Sir Charles Napier had issued the following signal to his command:'Lads, war is declared with a numerous and bold enemy. Should they meet us and offer battle, you know how to dispose of them. Should they remain in port, we must try and get at them, success depends on the quickness and precision of your firing. Also lads, sharpen your cutlasses and the day is your own.'

This signal was sharply criticised for its belligerent tone, but as events unfolded almost nothing of the sort predicted by Napier transpired, and the 1854 campaign in the Baltic was almost too quiet for the often frustrated sailors.

HMS *Archer*, Elsinore Sound, Monday April 3rd, 1854

My dearest parents

We have just anchored in Elsinore, the fleet we now hear are in Kioge Bay, a little to the southward of Copenhagen. It is blowing a gale of wind from the North so that perhaps we may run on this afternoon. It is blowing so hard here that no boat could land so that I shall not have the pleasure of seeing Elsinore this time; I hope we may be some time in Kioge Bay as then I should have a chance of seeing Copenhagen.

We have a most *miserable* crew, the dregs of Woolwich, lazy indolent dirty blaguards, neither soldiers, sailors, tinkers or tailors, fellows that have come to sea to live upon the sailors who do the work in a ship. We hardly can get a sail furled under an hour, but I think that we must improve, Captain Heathcote has the best temper I have ever seen on board ship.

The three Lieutenants have to do all the work. The deck is never to be left for a moment without one of us. Bathurst and myself keep the forenoon and middle afternoon and first watches, Forbes the morning, and 4 to 8.

Yesterday I was on deck 16 hours out of the 24, but I must say I like the ship notwithstanding. There is no getting out of temper with a man that never gets out of temper with any body, and if he does make you

The Baltic, 1854.

work hard has nothing but the good of the service at heart, not for the sake of bullying.

> Ever your loving son,
> S.G. Cresswell.

> The Ambasadors, Stockholm, April 8th, 1854

My dearest Parents

We arrived at a fort about 20 miles from here yesterday having left Elsinore the day after I wrote last. The next day we found the fleet anchored in Kioge Bay about 10 or 15 miles from Copenhagen, and the next day sailed for this place with dispatches.

The Government will not let us come up in the ship, so the dispatches were sent by Bathurst, who is evidently the favourite. Today he came down and I went up with the Captain who is a regular brick, and treats his officers as Gentlemen.

We had a sad accident today, saluting. One of our best men was blown to pieces. May God have mercy on his Soul.

Report says that tomorrow we are going to have a try at Cronstadt. Our ship is in poor order to fight at present but I think we shall do.

HMS *Archer*, Cruising off Filsund Light House, May 1854

My dearest parents

We remained at Stockholm 3 or 4 days, met the Admiral off Gotland. Unfortunately we nearly ran over the *Duke [of Wellington]*, or we should have had another trip to Stockholm, at least so he says, instead of which we were banished off here to cruise off Filsund light house on which unfortunate light house Bathurst is making some joke about our being black listed and sent to fill sand, we hope soon to be full but is seems to take a long time.

There is one good thing about it, it gives us a chance of getting our miserable crew a little clean, and in orders yesterday half the ship's company were scrubbed and today the other half. This is a great chance as it is probably the first time that soap and hot water have troubled them.

May 8th

Poor Poll who has again been in the list for some time I fear is bound for another world. It seems that he concealed his state at the Hospital in his anxiety to sail in the ship and left it still suffering from the effects of poison. He concealed his state for some time after we left England and when he went to the doctor it was too late for him to do much for him, parts of the stomach being seriously injured from the effects of the poison.

HMS *Archer*, Memel, May 18th, 1854

Dearest Parents

Here we are at Memel, a little Prussian port close to Russia. There is a very large trade here particularly with England.

It is with deep regret that I have to tell you of the death of poor Poll. He never recovered from the effects of the poison and poor fellow perhaps from a wish to be at his work, disguised his feelings.

We have lost 5 men since we left England. One at Stockholm, blown out of the port saluting; the other night in my watch one of our lookouts went over board and we did not succeed in picking him up, and I had reported the same man twice before to the Captain for being asleep on his look out.

What a ridiculous way the war is being carried on in, why do we not go in and attack some place of importance, or if we are not to do this why do they not send us home. We must be a tremendous expense to the country and are no use as the blockade is quite a farce.

We are placed under the order of Captain Kay (a very smart officer of 30) which I am very glad of as I have seen enough of our man to see that we shall do nothing by ourselves. He (our man) has been ground down for so many years that he has nothing left in his head except Station, Files and house maid's work at which he is first rate. Any man that has not a little originality of thought and action will do nothing here, nobody having any orders from the Commander in Chief.

HMS *Archer*, off the Gulf of Riga, June 1st

My dearest Parents,

I have just time to send you a line saying that I am well.

We did a very dashing thing the other day in the Gulf of Riga. What happened, *Archer* and *Conflict* ran in (under steam) full tilt for a place in the NE of the Gulf named Pernau. We were going to cut out vessels and play Old Harry with every body. However when we got within about 16 miles we either did, or we thought we heard a gun, and there is a report in the ship that an old woman with petticoats and a large dog was seen. I think it must be false for I do not think we could have seen 16 miles, but for our credit let us make it out that the old woman and the big dog was there as then the fact of our putting our helm up and running out of the Gulf faster than we came in will be fully accounted for with credit to all concerned.

What on earth are we all doing? One hundred ships in the Baltic and afraid to do the slightest thing. Is it that beautiful Government of ours, or is Sir Charles Napier afraid? I never took him for a coward although I do not admire him much.

Or is it that we wait for some final ships now at Kioge Bay in *very* bad order? If we do we make a grand mistake as we shall lose more by the time that the Emperor will gain, than we shall gain by two or three bad and undisciplined ships.

The honour and glory that will be due to the Baltic fleet if we go on in the same way will be something tremendous. Bathurst and I are not coming home in the Autumn unless we do something before then, probably shall run and join the Russians or Turks, quite indifferent which.

The frustration Cresswell felt in this letter about the lack of action in the Baltic was widely shared, and the age of Sir Charles Napier was blamed by some, while others blamed orders from the Admiralty. Sir Charles by all accounts presided over a very quiet campaign in 1854, with the taking of Bomarsund, in the Åland Islands the only major engagement, undertaken in August with the French, who had joined the British in the Baltic in June.

On 10 April *Amphion* and *Conflict* took Lebau without firing a shot, and destroyed the shipping in the Russian port. Cresswell in the *Archer* had no part in either action. Orders were sent from the Admiralty on 4 October, to attack Sveaborg, to the west of Helsinki on the Russian occupied Finnish coast. However, before the attack could be staged, the orders were cancelled on the 9th.

This vacillation has been attributed to a false rumour that Sebastopol had fallen to the Black Sea fleet, and to public pressure for more action against Russia. News that Sebastopol had not fallen caused the Sveaborg plans also to be cancelled. Sir Charles Napier's indecisiveness seems therefore at least in part the fault of a vacillating Admiralty, though his conduct, by at least one first hand account seems at the least hesitant, as described in Cresswell's letter of 28 October, below.

Whatever the case, Lord Palmerston took a robustly different view from the frustrations of the fleet, and its Commander. Speaking on the Naval Estimates in 1855, he said 'It is due to him to say that nothing has occurred in the course of the last year which in the slightest degree diminishes the high character which he has attained in the service of his country . . . He secured the country against all the evils which might have arisen if the Baltic fleet of Russia had been permitted to quit its ports and scour the sea.'

If the fleet's duties, as praised by Palmerston, but disliked by Cresswell and his fellow sailors, were the dull business of blockading, there were occasional diversions, like this description of an encounter by night off the Russian coast:

I will try and describe it. The *Archer* running under all stud sails, with the sails generally in dark shade but having portions of them, and the masts and rigging, lit up by the moon, showing clear.

The chase just distinguishable inshore, the sandy coast of Russia in the background showing white under the silvering influence of the moon, and every few minutes the beauty of the scene and the stillness of the night disturbed, but not destroyed by our monster gun vomiting forth 68 lbs of iron backed by 14 lbs of powder, shaking the whole ship and sending its echoes reverberating and grumbling along the enemy's coast.

The part of the coast along which we were running we knew little about but from soundings being laid down on the charts, so it was rather nervous work for the Master and 1st Lieutenant, the Captain being in his cot.

Shortly after 12, the darkest time; he outwitted us by taking in his sail. We thought he had run into some creek and hove to, as we lost sight of him. At daylight we sighted him about 6 miles further on and made all sail after him. But after two hours chase, and having gained on him so little, and he being close to his port (Lebau) we gave it up, having run 50 miles off our station, after a little cutter.

The only reason that we chased him so long was because we wanted his sails for deck clothes for the ship and expended £14 worth of powder and shot in trying to get sails that would value about £5. But it was a great lark and I am sure it did our crew £14 worth of good in the excitement it made.

HMS Archer, June 17th

My dearest mother

We sailed from Faro sound on the 15th with three of our prizes, the *Dauntless* having sailed the day before for England with the others. We met the *Valorous* at sea, which ship gave us the information of a most abominable cowardly attack by the Russians on some boats that had been sent in to some place in the Gulf of Bothnia with a flag of truce.

Memel, June 18th. We have just anchord in Memel so I must have this ready to send at a moment's notice.

HMS Archer, Faro Sound, July 1st

My dearest Mother

Here we are again at Faro. We met the *Amphion* the other day at sea. She had just come down from the Admiral who was at anchor with the screw line of battle ships about 30 miles from Cronstadt. We can't hear that he had any idea of making an attack.

Admiral Corry's squadron were off Hango Head [SW of Helsinki], where Sir Charles Napier is to join him. We have come here to tow a collier over to the fleet and take advantage of the confusion to fill up with coal and water, anchored this morning at 8 and sail this evening at 5.

I am so glad that you have been staying with Lord Cholmondeley.* I hope that my dear father will take a little more to gadding about than was his wont. It, I am sure will do you both good and break the monotony of your at present childless home. We all require excitement to keep us going.

You will excuse my writing more as I have a chance of getting a walk on shore but I must go at once as the boat is waiting.

HMS *Archer*, July 5th

My dearest Parents,

There is a report that we are to remain with the fleet, we are now with Admiral Corry. Sir Chas Napier is up near Cronstadt with the screw liners.

We are at cross purposes with respect to Captain Heathcote. Poor man he was confined to his cot for 3 weeks, the greater part of the time not able to move hand or foot, but I am glad to report his now being much better.

We are *just* in sight of the Russian fleet in Helsingfjord [Helsinki]. Yesterday we saw them loose sails. Three made sail, the blaguards won't come out although we have only 7 liners, and all sailing ships but one, and she no use as a steamer.

The report is that Sir C. Napier is so disgusted with the way he is humbled by our rotten Government that he has written to be superseded. If this is true I shall think well of him for ever after.

The longer I live in the world and the more I see of the service, the more I feel that the fact of gaining rank does not gain happiness.

Our poor Captain said the other day when he was stretched out perfectly helpless in his cot, 'Here I am having lived all my life amongst

---

* At Houghton Hall, built by Sir Robert Walpole, a few miles east of Kings Lynn, and Norfolk's leading stately home, still inhabited by the Cholmondeleys today.

holystones, sand and hard work, a Post Captain after having sacrificed everything to gain rank, and now having gained that that which I have always worshipped, I find myself the helpless object you see me.'

I have been thinking cooly and dispassionately for some time about my prospects. Ambition and vanity have left my nature for ever. My only wish for promotion now is the hope that it may enable me to live quietly on shore for the future.

If I am not promoted in 6 months I shall not be for 8 or 10 years taking the average chances.

HMS Archer, Memel, July 22nd, 1854

My very dear Parents

Young Wallace* will probably be sent home. He was regularly invalided, so that if his parents wish him to go into a hospital, and he prove a fit subject, he will get the best treatment for nothing. I should strongly recommend his friends *not* to let him go to sea again. I have little doubt that they will be able to get his discharge from the service without paying anything, if the circumstances are properly represented.

I feel much for the poor lad, and blame myself not a little for allowing his parents to over persuade me. I should have seen at a glance that he was quite unfitted for such a service. He sailed from Faro Sound in the *Dauntless* on the 14th for England, and probably will arrive there about the end of this month.

I have just been talking to Master Harry Hornigold.* He tells me he is all right, and I am glad to say he is turning out *very* well. He is a clean lad and has his full share of shrewdness and good sense. He is also a manly boy for his age and I have little doubt he will live to be a 1st class warrant Officer.

I shall get him into the Mizzen top as soon as I can, when he is a little stronger and older. At present I believe he is best as a gun room boy. Tell his parents that he wishes me to say that he is happy and well.

---

* Boys who, as family friends, had been found places in HMS *Archer* by Cresswell. Harry Hornigold was one of a family of fishermen at Kings Lynn who crewed the *Wild Duck*, the Cresswell family sailing boat. The association between the Cresswells and the Hornigolds lasted many generations, and in 1913 George Cresswell, SGC's nephew, and his wife sent two wreaths, a cross and an anchor, suitable for a sailor's grave, to a Hornigold funeral at Terrington, a fenland village not far from Lynn.

We have now got a day or two to paint &c. &c. and get a little clean. You would hardly know the ship again.

The weather has been very hot for the last week, quite uncomfortably so. I think the temperature in my cabin which is as cool a place as there is in the ship is up to 75°.

Charles Forbes and myself went on shore yesterday and went out to some gardens about three miles in the country. There happened to be a grand fete given to all the school children, I suppose there might have been 1,000 girls from 2 years to 16 or 17, not dressed in any uniform dress but all allowed to exercise their own taste.

Nearly all the girls were dressed in white of apparently to me, (who do not pretend to be a judge of ladies' dresses) very fine material.

Round the head they wore a chaplet of flowers, generally of a light blue. In the middle of the grounds a large piece of ground was enclosed for the little people to dance and sing.

You would be surprised to see four or five hundred of our country school girls dancing the waltz and gallop with inimitable grace. Some thousands of people were there of all sorts. All the little boys had to carry small flags and after playing about the grounds for some time, had to fall in and be drilled. I fancy this is done with the idea of encouraging a military spirit.

It was a very pretty sight and all the good people seemed to enjoy themselves very much, numbers of little parties eating and drinking under the trees. Forbes made a very true and sensible remark on seeing all this gaiety and happiness: These people live to enjoy life, We (the English) to make money or a name.

A message has just come off from the Captain to say we sail today.

I believe we go off to our old cruizing ground again.

HMS *Archer*, July 24th, 1854

My dearest Parents

We left Faro sound last on the 1st July with a coal barge in tow. In standing in shore off Filsund under steam and sail we very nearly got on shore. If we had I do not think we should have got off again.

As we were standing in the Master went down to the Captain and asked him to tack, but he thought we might wait until he came on deck. Nobody thought we were so near. I happened to ask the Master if I should send a hand in the chains, he said I had better. His first cast was

4 fathoms, next 3, and before we were round we could see the rocks close to us, just under water. We draw 15 feet, and there was a nasty heavy swell, so I will leave you to judge how near we must have been. If it had not have been for our steam we must have gone ashore as she would not have tacked.

From this place we could see the Russian fleet excercising, but they were too knowing to be tempted out although we had nothing but sailing ships.

I went on board the *St George* to dine with an old messmate and met Captain Eyres at dinner, he was most civil, regretting that he had not been able to come on board to see me as he had to go on to see the French Admiral's ship, almost too good a post Captain of a 120-gun ship coming two miles to see a Lieutenant, however it was very civil to say so.

He asked me to dinner for the next day, but the *Archer* to be at anchor for two days was quite out of the question.

We went to Faro sound after having spent the forenoon in excercising with the fleet (in which we did fairly) and coaled, weighed at midnight and came out again, anchoring in 30 fathoms water, (no joke of a heave).

Down came Sir Charles Napier from his cruize *not* to Cronstadt. It was a magnificent sight to see the steam fleet steam past us, that glorious ship the *Duke* leading, that ought by herself to take any battery in the world.

I hope that there is some chance of a brush now as I do not think the French would send out 30,000 troops for nothing although we send out 30 line of battle ships.

Sir Charles Napier sent us off to our station again, and Capt. Key was ordered up to the Admiral so that our Captain is senior officer. The first thing he did was to send the *Cruiser* off to Memel to take and get out letters, and then went into the Gulf of Riga. Off Downess, we saw 4 large boats at anchor. We anchored, and armed our boats and sent them in; Forbes in the lst Gig commanding, Bathurst in the Pinnace and myself commanding the two cutters. Pulled up in grand style and captured three fishing boats!

We then went on shore. The 3 Lieuts. and our 20 marines, broke open and went over the light houses. It was rather a good joke, but having sent the marines down to the boat we had nobody to break open the second light house, so we pressed two or three Russians who were standing about.

They did not much like the job, but showing them a pistol had the desired effect. We found nothing and went back to our boats.

As we were pulling off to the ship a cavalry officer rode down to the beach. Probably he had troops with him. If he had been down a quarter of an hour sooner he might with the greatest of ease have cut us off, as we were some way from our boats and had only 20 green Marines. After this glorious attack, we went out of the Gulf.

We then went around there and on the 16th gained intelligence from the Consul that a suspicious vessell, a Dutch Galliot the *Wilomena* by name was bound from Amsterdam to Pilau. We immediately weighed, I was on shore at the time and with some of my messmates was just sitting down to our dinner when an order came to go on board immediately so we lost our dinner and made the best of our way on board.

It was a very dense fog . . .

HMS *Archer*, at sea, July 26th

My dear Parents,

I think I left off just as we left Memel in a thick fog to go after a suspicious vessel bound from Amsterdam, to some of the Russian ports. We sailed on the 17th and anchored on the 18th (the fog still as thick as possible) by the head, thinking we must be near Pilau. 10 minutes after our anchor had been let go the fog cleared a little, it was my watch, when the cry 'Sail Ho!' ran over the ship. To be away in the cutter was the work of a few moments, and as we had a fair wind I was soon aboard my gentleman who was at the time making the best of his way into the ports.

The Captain had told the name of the suspected vessel, the *Wilomena*; the first question I asked (was) 'What is your vessel's name?' The *Wilomena* all right. 'Put your helm down and go alongside HMS *Archer*.'

The first cask we hoisted out was all sorts of chain gear, I believe appertaining to cavalry, after this we found 12 or 15 more casks of it. Now if this can be proved to be for the Russian army, as I believe it can, she will be a prize to us to the value of about £10,000.

We put a Prize crew on board and sent her into Pilau. The Capt. has written to the Admiral about her. After this we steamed back to Memel in about as thick a fog as we went down, anchored for one night then went off to join the *Cruiser* and *Conflict*, then went to Faro, and are now back again with *Conflict*. I believe we sail immediately for Memel.

HMS *Archer*, Memel, July 31st, 1854

My dear parents

We are now back in Memel, we sailed last night at 7 o'clock for the Courland squadron, but meeting a vessel from Riga, took her, and towed her back here. She is a little Dutch sloop of about 80 tons, in ballast, not much of a prize if she should prove one, but every little helps.

It is very jolly the 5 prizes being confirmed. I have bought some rather pretty things here, Bohemian glass, Saxon table cloth &c. on the strength of the prize money. I shall send them home by the first chance.

We can't understand what the French troops are coming out for, it is so late in the year. I think we have made a regular mess of the war in the Baltic. I am sick of it as far as the war goes, our little ship is comfortable enough, the Captain is a real good fellow, we get on very well on the whole, sometimes we have a little growl, but as he generally hauls down his colours first and goes off deck, it is rather amusing than otherwise.

He is still very seedy; if he was a wise man he would give up Glory and go home to that little wife of his and be nursed. I am very glad to hear that the sketches* are done so well, pray send me a copy out. There is no difficulty in sending them. There is a steamer that runs from Hull to Memel very often. My tailor sent me out some clothes the other day by her.

Bathurst and myself have been sailing a little in the cutter's dinghy &c. The other night we went away in the dinghy (a little fast boat about 10½ feet long & 5 broad) to smoke our backeys, and commenced working to windward, or rather trying to do so. Then we woke up to the fact of our being about 1½ miles dead to leeward of the ship with a very nasty head sea. It was a cruel state of affairs as it was after dinner. However there was no help for it and so we bravely set to work and pulled up, although several times we nearly gave it up as a bad job and were for bearing up for Riga.

We are now on our way to Memel; last night we went into Windau, and Bathurst went in to see if he could cut anything out. He returned on board with a very nice new gig and a fine large boat.

---

* Cresswell's eight sketches of the *Investigator's* Arctic voyage had been published as a set of lithographs dedicated to Queen Victoria.

August 5th

We have been close to Riga, but unfortunately it came on to blow so very hard on shore, that we all had to beat out again to save ourselves from being driven on shore. We hear from the vessels which have come out of Riga that the Russians have 16 Gun boats there, and that there are many troops about the place. The crews are *very* bad and the boats not good, being too light for the heavy guns that they carry. I wish we might have a brush with them but I fear there is no such good luck.

We are now at anchor off Buno Island with the *Conflict* and the *Cruiser*.

The Captains of the ships that have just come out of Riga tell as there is much discontent amongst the people, and that there would be a Revolution in any other country but Russia.

HMS *Archer*, August 13th, 1854

My dear Parents,

I will try and continue my *Archer* news from the time the *Conflict* sailed for Memel with my last letter. After she had left us we anchored off Buno, about 8 miles from it. On Sunday we made a sort of picnic party to go there, Forbes, Cooper our paymaster, Thruppe of the *Cruiser* and myself. The two captains also went in their gigs but did not join our party.

We landed on the right hand side of the island and walked through the trees towards the left end. The walk was really most beautiful in a sort of natural avenue. The trees were much finer than any I have seen out here before, and the variety greater although the fir predominates.

This island originally belonged to the Swedes, and it seems that they have never intervened with the Russians that have been sent there. A few weeks ago the Russians (I believe only about 10 in number) left the island. The present inhabitants are a very fine race of people, the men markedly handsome and the women very ugly, but good tempered healthy looking frows.

The houses are built of rough trees laid one on the other, the chinks filled in with a sort of clay cement and the tops thatched over. They all have stoves made out of hardened clay, I think these will give much more heat than the open English stoves.

The rooms of the houses are very large but I fancy two or more families live in one. There is a pastor in the place and a most primitive but pretty little Church.

I made them understand that I wanted eggs and milk and in a few minutes was surrounded by women with from 2 to 50 eggs each. These we bought, but they did not seem to care about money, I fancy they hardly knew the value of it. We had not forgotten the inward man and with eggs and milk, a bottle or so of Champagne &c &c we made a very jolly dinner under the trees, and with the assistance of tobacco got on board at 9 o'clock in high good humour with ourselves and all mankind after the most pleasant day I have spent since I have been in the Baltic.

I dined with Douglass who is an old mess mate of mine the other day.

He is a young man and was in the days of the *Agincourt*, considered a great goose, but the fact of his being an Hon. and having married Sir W. Parker's daughter has made him a Commander and a damned clever fellow to boot.

HMS *Archer*, Memel Harbour, August 23rd, 1854

My dearest Parents

Huzza, Captain at last! The Captain having gone to Pilau and Forbes with him, he is better, also the Doctor and Paymaster; Bathurst has sailed for England in charge of three prizes, so that the Master and myself are the only officers on board.

As I have, or rather take, a little spare time as Captain, I will continue our adventures. We went down to a place called Sackenbaum, 30 miles to the North of Lebau, and anchored within about a mile of the shore.

We soon saw some cavalry soldiers ride down; many women and children were also setting about. We waited until four or five of the troops were together, and no women or children to be seen in the way and let fly a shell which burst just over them, but I hope a few yards too far, as we could not make out that any body was hurt (I trust no women or children).

After this feat we rose anchor, and steamed towards Memel. The next day we boarded a vessel I told you of in my last. The next day we took two vessels, one a brig and the other a bark, bound from Spain to Memel, 60 miles to the North of Memel. Their papers were all correct.

The way they accounted for being so far to the Northward was that there had been southerly winds; we had southerly winds too, but light and fine weather. I have little doubt that they were trying to land their cargoes on the coast of Russia. I took the brig in tow and sent a prize crew in the bark.

That night in a tremendous squall, we being at the time under whole topsails and top gallant sails, bang went fore and main topmasts and the mizzen T'Gallant mast, mizzen topmast only a *little* sprung and a nice job we had of it to get to rights again. Tomorrow I am going to holystone decks, and in the evening give a ball to Memel.

All our best men have had leave, and to confirm their character they all instantly on landing got drunk, and commenced fighting every body and were put in chokey.

I only got them out today. There is a request from the head man here not to send more than five on shore at one time, that if we do they will have to send for the military to protect the place. This does not say much for the strength of Memel.

HMS *Archer*, off Memel, October 5th

My dear Parents

I write this to send by the very first chance, as I fear you may get an exaggerated account of the sickness on board; I told you of 60 of our men having been left on shore for some days, they mostly behaved *very badly* many of them drunk the whole time, sold all their clothes & sleeping about in that state &c &c. The result is that they brought off a little cholera from which one has died. There is only one other bad case, and there are great hopes for him.

There has been a good deal of diarrhoea in the ship, a good deal of it sham I think, fellows think it a good chance to get in the list for a skulk. It is a hard thing for the doctor to discriminate in, and as he says it is better to put two well men in the list for a day or two, than keep one ill man out; we have now lame and lazy about 35 sick. There are no more dreaded cases of cholera, and as we have now been 6 days from Memel I hope we shall not. Master Hornigold has had a sharp attack of diarrhoea but now is much better.

Our poor Master I fear is going fast (not with Cholera); a general break up of constitution; I firmly believe if we could have sent him home some time back he would have recovered, but these gales of wind are enough to kill a weak man, let alone an ill.

Thank God I am quite well, I have not put a grain of medicine down my throat since I left England, and do not intend to if I can help it.

We are just a little quiet now which gives me a chance of writing this, nothing but knocking and rolling about; we had a few hours fine last Sunday, and took advantage of it to run into Lebau to land the poor fellows that we took from the Russian boats (20 of them). I went on shore with a flag of truce, the whole town turned out to see us, I should much have liked to have gone up into the town, but as the Burgomaster came to meet me, I had no excuse, I have run enough risks in that way.

This cruising now is frightful work, not as far as danger goes, for that is a thing that does not much trouble me, but for monotony and discomfort, eternally struggling off a lee shore, always at sea, always in a gale of wind; but it, like all bad and all good things must have an end, but I fear it will not be so soon as you expect, I do not think we shall go home until December.

By the time you receive this, I trust you will have seen some of the Investigators.

Some of my messmates have got hold of a report that the *Phoenix* had stuck in the ice, and not been able to get on. I do not think this can be the case or I should have heard of it from you.

October 7th

There is a slight change in the weather since last night, as now it rains instead of blowing. Since I was last writing we have had a very heavy gale, under close reefed main topsail, Main Trysail & Fore staysail; two days never go over but we are reduced to this sail.

We are now standing into Memel to pick up our boats, men and letters.

Our poor Master is much the same, that poor fellow that I spoke about is sinking fast, and we have another rather bad case, but on the whole are much better, the sick list decreased to 26.

HMS *Archer*, Faro, October (23rd), 1854

My dear Parents

I was knocked down yesterday by seeing that William Cresswell* had died of Cholera on board a transport, only the night before the troops

---

* Cresswell's first cousin.

landed. I fear it is too true, my poor dear Aunt, how will she ever bear up against such a blow, I do most deeply feel for her and them all at Cresswell, and poor Ada too, being left a widow under such circumstances is dreadful.

Our poor master died the day before yesterday, and yesterday we buried him in a little tumble-down Swedish church yard, a place of no pretensions but a quiet place to rest.

I am glad to tell you that the Cholera has quite left us although we still have rather a large sick list.

The *Duke* has been here for a day or two to coal, on her way to the southward. There is the greatest discontent in the fleet at nothing having been done.

Report says that nearly all the Captains have cut Admiral Charles, his conduct on several occasions has been nothing short of cowardly.

HMS *Archer*, at sea, October 28th

My dear Parents

We have been in a continual gale of wind since my last letter, with the exception of a few hours, in which we gave the *Amphion* some provisions that we had brought over from Faro.

She then started for Faro, I imagine her going to Faro must have been the reason for our bringing provisions from Faro to her with the chance of 20 to one that we should not be able to communicate. However she had taken a magnificent prize, a cutter with two men and a woman which Mr Captain Admiral Key* succeeded in nearly drowning by towing the cutter under water.

The lively but ungallant Russian gentlemen got up by the hawser, and the fair one might have met with a watery grave, had it not been for one of the seamen. This proved a good thing for us as he, Key, has turned the Russians over to us, for a passage down to Memel.

We always like going to Memel, as it gives us a chance of getting late letters and papers.

That old humbug Sir Charles Napier is off. He anchored off Faro for a day to coal. A second master has joined us as Master from the *Duke*. He says that all Sir Charles does is to sit between two stoves in his cabin rolled up in fur and he is, or makes out that he is, very seedy.

---

* Satirical reference by SGC to Captain Astley Cooper Key.

I am thankful to say that the Cholera has quite left us.

October 29th

We have just got in and I have got the Good news of my promotion.
I shall not be able to leave the ship until we hear of it officially, and I fear
not then unless there is interest used for my discharge.

HMS *Archer*, Memel, October 31st

My dear Mother

We are just going out of Memel, so I shall send this in by the pilot. I
fear it is the last time you will hear from me for some time, as report says
we are not to come to Memel again, and we shall not go to Faro, as we
are complete with water, coals and provisions.

Most likely I shall get my promotion officially when we next go to
Faro. In that case I shall go home in the first ship, most likely I shall land
at Copenhagen and find my way overland.

How awful the news about Franklin and his party.* I was more shocked
at it than I ever remember being about any thing in my life. I did not know
I *could feel so much*. In fact the late events, first the return of Mr M'Clure,
then our poor master's death, then the sad news from the Crimea, now my
promotion and this discovery about Franklin have half turned my head.

God bless you all my dearest mother and grant that we may soon meet
in safety.

P.S. I had young Hornigold on shore with me yesterday. He is hard up
for under clothing in this cold weather. I am trying what I can do
for him and am having a warm monkey jacket made for him on
shore here.

HMS *Archer*, at sea, November 6th

My dearest Parents,

We have had three days of gale of wind in the last week, and we are all
heartily sick of this cruising. I do not believe there is a chance of this ship
going home before the end of December, as there is not a sign of the frost

---

* Confirmation from Capt John Rea, Arctic explorer, of the death of Sir John
Franklin, and loss of his expedition.

setting in yet, and such places as Windau and Lebau, from being so exposed must be late before they freeze over. You may fancy how I long to get home as this is all lost time to me, the only advantage is the £40 a year difference between Lieutenant's full pay and Commander's half pay.

I have sounded the Captain to try and find out if there is any chance of his letting me go, when he hears officially of my promotion, but I fear not as he has not *an order* for my discharge. I can't much blame him so many of our officers being away in prizes.

I have written to Barrow* about it, and also to Ozzard, Sir Charles Napier's secretary, and an old friend and messmate of mine in the *Agincourt*. So now I have done all I can, I must let it bide.

HMS *Archer*, at sea, running for Memel, November 20th

My dear parents

I much fear not that I shall not be able to get out of the ship before she goes home, and in that case I shall not see you before the end of December. Nobody now thinks we shall leave this a day before the 15th of next month, I do not think before the 20th, as we can't go before all the Russian ports are frozen up.

We are all wild to hear more from Sebastopol, our last news from England is only up to the 3rd.

The weather is very cold and raw, much snow and hail but very little frost and the everlasting gales from the North and East instead of Westerly.

HMS *Archer*, off Faro, November 30th

My dearest Parents

We are now just about to go into Faro. Since I last wrote we have been up to Capt. Watson's Squadron, we did not communicate except by signal, so I did not hear if they had any official news for me, or not. The only signal he made to us was to go to Faro and join *Amphion*. Key may have my discharge. If he has, I shall not leave a stone unturned to get out of this ship, I fear the Captain will try to keep me if he can.

We have had a very heavy gale of wind from the SSW, and were blown into the mouth of the Gulf of Finland. We have now 16 hours dark, so our position was anything but pleasant.

---

* Sir John Barrow, Admiralty Secretary.

11 PM: We anchored in the mouth of Faro harbour at 5 this morning, it being too dark to go further, so we have not yet heard the news. It is quite a treat to be at anchor after such a knocking about.

The Captain told me tonight that if I get official intelligence of my promotion he would let me go if Captain Watson would give him a mate to do my duty; Captain Watson not being here, I do not think this is much of a chance.

P.S. The report is that we are going home almost immediately.

HMS *Archer*, at sea, December 4th

My dear Parents

We are at last on our first stage home. We sailed from Faro yesterday, and expect to be at Elsinore the day after tomorrow. Captain Watson came in before we left Faro, but would not let me go, so I must take my chance in the ship!

I should think we shall be home by the 15th. I shall cut and run the instant we arrive whether the Captain likes it or no, I have had quite enough grinding.

I received an Admiralty letter from the *Amphion*, announcing my promotion. Also some very *old* letters dated 23 Oct, one from Charlie, one from my Father. If your had sent them by Memel I would have got them on the 29th October, six days old, instead of one month and ten days. The *Conflict* has gone to Memel to get the body of Captain Foote,* and she will bring any letters that may be there, but you must not write there after receiving this.

We have left our station 15 days before I expected.

Elsinore, Friday 1 A.M.

My dearest parents

I am off for Copenhagen at 8.30 this morning so I must wind up. We had a fair passage down here, anchored at 3 last evening. The report is that we remain here till all the ships are on their way home, and that the old Admiral is coming to have a look at us in a steamer.

---

* Capt. John Foote was the commander of HMS *Conflict*, drowned with four men in the ship's gig, off Memel on 18 April.

We had some most dirty work working between Bornholm and the mainland, again a strong gale from the SW; however here we are all safe and I trust to, D.V. in a few days be with you my dearest parents.

HMS *Archer*, Elsinore, Tuesday

My dearest Parents,

This will be my last letter from the Baltic, as we sail tomorrow morning wind and weather permitting for *Leith*.

The Capt. has been very jolly, and excused me from duty while we are in this place, but I shall have to keep watch on the passage home, as here are so few officers he will trust.

My plan will be on arrival to get leave from the Captain and bolt to Cresswell or elsewhere, perhaps home, and if they get hold of me then I shall be rather mistaken.

I am now on shore, writing with just light enough not to see in a dirty pot shop, the best hotel in the place, a miserable thawey rainy drizzly foggy day. I came on shore to get my washed clothes, and shall be heartily glad to get off when I can get a boat.

I have no words to tell how I long to see you all.

HMS *Archer*, December 19th

My dearest Parents

We are having a very bad passage, nothing but N Westerly winds until yesterday when we got a gale from the NE. But we had got so far to the southward that we could but just lay our course under steam and sail, and driving the ship against a head sea, six or seven miles an hour she made wet work of it, and I consider we may think ourselves fortunate only to have lost a Fore Top Gallant mast Staysail. We shall be about 220 miles off today, but as the wind has come a little ahead again, I fear we shall not fetch in by tomorrow.

> Ever your loving Son
> S. Gurney Cresswell

P.S. December 23rd, 8 P.M.

My dearest Parents

It is a great disappointment not being able to be with you on Xmas day, but the fates have decided against it, we are not yet in and shall not be until tomorrow, so there is no chance of my being able to get home by that time. So I intend if we get in early tomorrow to spend this Xmas day at Cresswell and come on the next.

For Cresswell the Baltic campaign personified the tedium of some aspects of naval life; his view of blockade duty was clear, despite the occasional excitements of chasing or seizing ships aiding the enemy, and the bounty which flowed from these rare events. Whether from his own character or under restrictive orders from home, Sir Charles Napier gave his fleet little to do.

Nevertheless, Cresswell received his promotion from Lieutenant to Commander for his part in the Baltic service, which laid the basis for the next phase of his career.

FOUR

HMS *Sparrowhawk, April–August 1856*

The year 1855 was largely spent by Cresswell at the Naval College at Portsmouth. Like many young officers, he periodically returned to shore stations, and had already spent some months at the gunnery training school, HMS *Excellent*, in 1848. His parents took a house at Southsea for a few weeks to see him and his colleagues.

Admiral Sir Thomas Cochrane, Cresswell's former commander in the China Seas, was Port Admiral at the time, and Mrs Cresswell records meeting him. He was 'very courteous, and showed us many features of interest at Admiralty House.' Nonetheless, she was not as enthusiastic as Cresswell about Cochrane, and she writes 'I never lost my feeling that there was something "not sound at the core", about the Admiral.

This is in contrast to Cresswell's enthusiasm for Sir Thomas, whose command of the China fleet he was later to compare favourably with that of Admiral Sir Michael Seymour on the same station in 1858. In fairness to Sir Michael, perhaps an Admiral, seen and respected by a 16-year-old apprentice, is likely to win the comparison with the same office holder viewed by the captain of a ship with many years' experience.

All the same, it is a feature of the frankness of Cresswell's letters home that they are full of outspoken commentary on the admirals, captains and other authorities who, at greater or lesser distance, ruled the life of the ships and their crews. Naturally, the Admiralty at home comes in for some of the sharpest criticism. This was to become a major issue during Cresswell's second period of service in the China Seas, but his immediate destiny was nearer home. It was to give him his first taste of sole responsibility for a ship.

In February 1856, Cresswell was appointed to his first full command, the steam and sail dispatch vessel, HMS *Sparrowhawk*, of the Channel Fleet.

HMS *Sparrowhawk*, at sea off Dungeness, April 11th (1856)
Dearest Parents

The screw goes thump thump thump, and the ship's old stern and therefore the cabin of the Captain and with the cabin of the Captain the Captain himself goes shake shake shake, so that you must excuse bad writing.

We left Chatham 2 days before I intended through a mistake of the Captain Superintendent. The ship is in a beastly state of unreadiness, not even having our boats. They were sent after us to Sheerness.

Monday afternoon and Tuesday morning, received 105 tons of coal. Tuesday afternoon made a frantic effort to clean ship. Wednesday received Powder, Shell and Water.

Thursday 3 P.M. sailed.

6 P.M. Blowing hard from the Westward, low barometer, looking greasy, ugly sunset; 7 hove to in the Downs.

Friday 5 A.M. Weighed. Weather more moderate, barometer risen.

So you see we are jogging on, the ship going 8 knots with a fresh head wind. As far as I can judge she behaves well on the whole, but we are all very green at present and two-thirds of us sea sick.

I am going to make a grand speech to the men, but I fear sea sickness would prevent its having the desired effect at present.

A steamer is a beastly thing, after all it is almost impossible to keep one's hands or ship clean. You will have seen by the papers that the review is put off till the 22nd or 23rd.*

I think the ship will knock about a good deal, but her motion is easy, she bends to the seas. It is a very pleasant sensation, something like being on a water bed.

(Spithead) April 14th

I anchored here on Friday night at 6 o'clock and on Saturday shifted berth. I am well and jolly.

Something has gone wrong in the engine, and I fear we shall have to

---

* The grand Spithead Review for Queen Victoria.

go into dock to repair. This is a great bore. I am very much taken up with going from the Northern Bank and Portsmouth harbour, and have to go in again now. Young Foster of Norwich is on board, so I must cut this short.

> Your loving son,
> S.G. Cresswell

HMS *Sparrowhawk*, off Ryde, April 28th, 1856

My dearest parents

I went on shore on Saturday to Portsmouth, and yesterday morning it rained so hard that I should have got wet if I had attempted to get on board, and therefore remained on shore. This is the reason why I did not write my usual Sunday letter.

In the first place I must tell you something about the Grand Naval Review, it was more a wonderful than a beautiful sight. Fancy a large manufacturing town under weigh. I had Harriet and Isabella and Cynthia Calthorpe on board, Tumps and Capt. Warren.

Tumps came on board the day before and made himself very jolly.

I think the young Ladies liked themselves, and on the whole that my part of the play went off well.

You will see all that the fleet did in the papers much better than I can explain it.

The *Royal George* (101 guns) and the *Duke of Wellington* (131 guns) were the two leading ships. Then came all the liners, then the frigates, then sloops then paddle steamers, then the flotilla of Gun boats and last but not least (in my opinion) the Despatch vessells. The floating batteries, mortar boats, &c forming a line from the Stokes Bay to Southsea Castle, the two lines of ships extended over 5 miles in length. The Queen came out of harbour, passed to the northward and entered the lines at the Western extreme and steamed through them; as soon as she had passed the Gun boats, they weighed and steamed in two lines after her; two pivot ships were anchored near the Castle, the Gun boats diverging to starboard and port around them.

Then the liners and all the rest weighed and followed the Gun boats as far as rounding the pivot ships. The Gun boats then went in and had a sham fight with Southsea Castle and the mortar boats and batteries.

I did not see my way very clearly at one time as to how I was to land the ladies, but a luck would have it, just as I was in despair, they signalled us to proceed to the Northern Bank.

That night there was a grand ball at Southsea to which *I did not go*, not much credit to me as I was dead tired.

The next night there was a grand ball here given to the flotilla in return for one given by the White division. The Calthorpes went, but as they did not do 'round abouts' I fear found it slow.

I fell dreadfully in love and remained so for 24 hours afterwards, with a Miss Ashton, good family, lots of tin &c., but as she was off the coast next day I blew off my superfluity of steam and banked my fires up.

I want a little more excitement than sticking here. I have been in such a glorious whirl lately that any ordinary proceedings are tame and insipid. I think I could exist in Borneo and the Indian archipelago for a year or so.

I believe we are to go into harbour in a few days to make good a few slight defects and then the gunboat flotilla are to have a sort of yachting cruize round England, after that if we prove ourselves fair sea boats some of us (the despatch vessels) are to go to India. I pray I may be one.

I hope to be able to get up to Town for a day or two shortly and shall make a point of calling on the Duke and Duchess of Northumberland and Sutherland, and also of having my thing-em-ebobs taken for you. You must give Charlie credit for having buttered me like mad to have it done.

[To his brother, William Cresswell]

HMS *Sparrowhawk*, off Ryde Pier, May 1st, 1856

My dear Bill

You see that I commence this on May day, and a pretty May day it is, raining and blowing like the very duce, and you may thank your stars that it is, as if it was not I should be peacocking some hen instead of writing to you.

I went to a stunning ball here the other night in the club house. It has a fine ball room facing the sea with a balcony. The balcony was shut in by a slight blind.

After having valsed and galoped with an angel, and finished the last galop, we took our seats in the balcony, when to the young ladies' surprise, by the pull of a string we were looking out onto the Solent. It was a lovely morning, calm and mild, the fleet in the distance, about half daylight, and the perfect calmness of the scene contrasted with the glare, the beauty and the clash of music within.

Byron maintained that there was only one in his time who could face Aurora after a ball. I have found another, however as she went away next day, I wish I had never seen her (but she was scrumptious).

I think we are slowly getting into order in the *Sparrowhawk*. The day before yesterday I was ordered to have my steam up by daylight the following morning as the blue division were ordered round to Plymouth.

At 9 o'clock Capt Yelverton came alongside and informed us that it was a mistake and that we were to remain behind for a trial trip.

If it would not blow so abominably I should go into the harbour today, to see the Capt. of the Fleet about it.

Yelverton and all the blue division have gone round to Plymouth so I fancy that I shall go after I have been tried. How lovely Plymouth will be, the Father can tell you how stunning it was in May 1842. (I was a miserable little youngster then.)

I know the Edens, and shall make lots of friends I do not doubt, the only thing I fear is that they should keep in the Sound, that would be too bad . . .

The Isle of Wight is exquisite; nothing in the world can be so beautiful as an English spring. There was no spring last year, but this is a good old fashioned spring, and if it had only been fine today, I am sure the May-ers would not have looked far for flowers and green things.

This is what I have yearned after since I have been at sea, to see my dear old country doff its gloomy colours and don its rich mantle of green (poetic, rather).

I think you know me well enough my dear Bill to see that I am just now looking at things through a bright fashion, the bright fashion is (on the whole) a much more happy and contended mind. I have arrived at this state through a refined philosophy.

The gist of it is this: Take it cooly, be thankful and contented with your position in life, and do not think of those above you, but those below when you want to measure up your place in the world. Enter into society and do not lose a ball or a good dinner. Do not drink bad wine as it affects the stomach, and the stomach the head. And lastly do not be such a muff as to hold a girl's hand without squeezing it.

If we are all alive and kicking in about 3 years will you be game to accompany me on such a cruize on the continent. That will be after my return from Borneo.

By the by I met a Capt. Brooke and an old messmate of mine, a

Dodey [nick name] Grant, who left the service to join Brooke in Borneo. They have both just returned, such real trumps, but young Grant, whose eldest brother is dead, danced rather too much with my enchantress of the dawn.

I fear that I shall not be able to get to town for the present to have my picture taken for the mother. I should wish to be with you if I wished for any change, which I do not.

I fear I do not make a good Captain. I dislike details too much, and am not strict enough. I would almost rather be bullied myself, than bully an officer.

I continue to like Pringle much. He wants experience a little, and has not a straight eye, but on the whole I consider myself most fortunate in having him. Tell the Mother I have received a letter from my Lady Calthorpe full of no end of thanks for taking the little Calthorpes on board the day of the Review.

I fear you are rather seedy, but I hope the dear Mother has exaggerated your indisposition. Fancy my not, out of five brothers, having one on board for the review.

HMS *Sparrowhawk*, off Ryde, Sunday May 4th, 1856

My dearest Parents

I wrote such a tearing letter to Bill two days ago that I have little to say now. On Friday I went in to try and find out something about our movements. The old Admiral hardly was aware of the existence of such a bird, and I did not find any thing satisfactory till I got hold of Mr Murray, who informed me that some time this week we should go into harbour and have another screw put in and that then we shall have twice the measured thrust.

After that I should think we should go round to Plymouth, as the rest of the blue division have gone round.

I am still several men short, but will not be in a hurry to fill up as there must be a great many men thrown on shore shortly by ships being paid off and then one will be able to pick and choose.

The red division of gun boats gave a grand ball at Ryde on Friday night. I was asked and of course went. We kept it up till 6.

Some Southsea people were there. I suppose you will be glad to hear of my having sailed for Plymouth (you may make yourselves quite easy as I now am a philosopher)

I am quite enjoying the English spring. We have had some rather cool nasty days lately, but today again is lovely and the Isle of Wight too beautiful.

I am going on shore this afternoon to smoke cigars and pick primroses &c. Will not Plymouth be beautiful . . .

I fear I shall not see any of our family again before I sail. Charlie, who is most kind in every way proposes to come up to Town to meet me there, but if we go to Plymouth, I fear I could not get up, it is so far.

This doing the Great Mogul is a funny life, sitting all day cloistered in our cabin, with a lot of jolly fellows, whose merry party I can't join, nor can they join my solitude.

In these solitary hours I devote myself to those philosophical principles which at present are not sufficiently defined to give them publicity.

I can't for the life of me think of any thing more to say,

P.S. You must allow that if one has no sense to write about and must write, one must write nonsense.

So I hope you will pardon some of the above.

P.P.S. I don't much fancy the account you give of the close shave you made of the edge of the cliff. Thank God that you did not come to any harm, pray take care of yourselves.

> H.M.S. *Sparrowhawk,*
> with her bow pointed into the basin waiting
> for the tide to be at the proper height to
> go in, raining very hard, trim weather for
> young ducks

May 22nd, 1856

My dearest Father

I have the most positive orders from Aunt Fanny to write immediately, and as I always obey orders from my superiors, here goes . . .

We came into harbour the day before yesterday and today are to go into the basin to get our other screw in, and make good some defects. There are several things adrift connected with the engine, and if they do not dock us now they will have to do so before we start for a long sea cruize.

I think I told you in my last that we are all to go out under Capt. Watson, for a excercising cruize, to look for a gale of wind &c. &c. But I do not think this will take place for 10 dys or so, as many of the Despatch Vessels want much doing to them.

Do not make so sure of our going to India. All I know about it is that there is a (most vague) report that some of these vessels are to go.

I hope you may be home before I start, how delightful it would be to be a few days together with my ship under our lea to talk over.

Now my dear father I must give you my very best thanks for your most handsome offer.

I believe you can get quite as good a chronometer for £50 now as you could in your sea days for £70 or £75.

There was a grand review of the troops here last Tuesday, the Queen inspected them. It was a most lovely day, they say about 30,000 people on the Common. I was in harbour just in time to see some of it from the ramparts (just over the gate going into Portsmouth). Looking down from them it was really a most beautiful and gay scene.

All the College commanders have now got ships with the exception of young Charles.

Several are appointed to ships two or more years in commission in room of officers promoted.

Their appointments accompanied by the most extraordinary letter from the Secretary saying that when the ships paid off they were not to consider that they had *any claim* for further employment because they had been afloat. . . .

I dine with Sir Geo. Seymour* tomorrow. I believe he gives good dinners, but not so grand as our friend Sir T.C. I hear that he, Sir T.C. is as grand as ever in Belgrave Square.

I am going to ask leave to go to Town for the fireworks on the 29th, and as I am asked to the Northumberland at homes during May, they being on Wednesdays, and the 28th being Wednesday, I believe I shall go up on that day if I can, and honour Northumberland house. I have had a most warm invitation to stay with the John Hay Gurneys during the fun. I intend to accept it if I go.

---

* Commander at Portsmouth, successor to Sir T Cochrane.

HMS *Sparrowhawk*, Plymouth, July 12th, 1856

My dearest Father

Now to answer your questions. The *Sparrowhawk* was out in the gale. We were just in the chops of the channel. I should not have called it a violent gale although it blew very hard with us, we had the wind from the WNW and it gradually worked round to NNW; during the first part of the gale we were under Whole Gaff Foresail, Foresail and Spanker and thrashed the other two ships all to nothing, they having single reefed foresail and mainsail and staysail.

I then expecting bad weather took in my spanker, 3 reefs in Gaff foresail and two in Main sail and set it so that I had a reef in my main sail and 2 in my foresail more than they had. Under these circumstances they beat me a little. Towards evening the weather looking finer, I shook the reefs out of the fore and main sail and ran up to my friends like a shot who had now bore up and shaped a course for Falmouth. We did not go into Falmouth but still kept away for this place (Plymouth), a strong gale behind us at one time going 11½ knots. The screw was up during the whole time.

I believe that these vessels would ride out any gale hove to with a close reefed mainsail or main Trysail and Fore staysail.

We of course took a little water in over the bows &c. but nothing to speak of.

She rolls a goodish few if we have not sail to steady her, but it is an easy roll on the whole, she is not half as bad as the *Archer*.

I think we have discovered what causes the clattering with the screw, we have at all events discovered a way of locking the engine that prevents it.

I was cruising about amongst the squadron in the sound at 12 o'clock last night. You will ask how was that.

I went alongside the coal hulk to fill up at 3 P.M. being 34 tons short and she being nearly empty we had to work the coal aft from the fore part of her hold and then had no end of a hoist. I have the greatest horror of coaling and coal hulks, so I made them finish the job off, which they did by 11.30 and then went back to my own billet. Today is cleaning day but the ship is so dirty we should have a cleaning week.

There was an order out here that all Gun vessels and Gun boats should send all the men that can be spared under charge of the officer commanding the said vessel or boat on board the senior officer ship in the sound to Church on Sunday.

This I considered infra dig so went on shore and sent some men with Pringle. By some fluke the Admiral thinks that I, with two or three more despatch commanders were the only officers who obeyed the order, and he has written to the Admiralty reporting the Lieuts commanding Gun boats for not being present. At the same time he has cancelled the order as it relates to Commander's commands and says it was never intended to include them.

H.M.Yacht* *Sparrowhawk*, off Osborne, August 10th

My dearest Father,

We came here from Cowes yesterday in the afternoon.

We are in hourly expectation of being off. We go the Channel Islands first (I believe) and then to Plymouth. After that it depends on circumstances. There is a report we go to Lisbon and Madeira but I don't think it likely myself . . .

Was it not a tremendous bore missing my ship. She just missed running down a schooner coming round going 10½ knots. The master told me it was the nearest thing he ever saw. He had gone below for a minute when he heard the cry of a sail close to. He flew up and put the helm over and just shaved her. We should have cut her right in two as sure as fate if we had struck her going that pace.

So that in this case I am a fortunate man, as if we had run her down there would have been an enquiry, and then it would be 'where was the Captain?' There would have been the devil to pay and no pitch hot enough and no mistake.

Pringle reported my not being on board when he arrived on Wednesday morning. The Admiral [Sir Geo Seymour] did not seem quite to wake up to the fact.

Next morning I went to see him. Marched in expecting him to open fire (I had sent to say I wanted to speak to him). However, as I thought it would be a pity to broach a disagreeable subject I had nothing to say. So after staring at one another for a minute he asked me if I was ready, and I said yes, and made my bow.

Yesterday there was a most splendid yacht race, blowing a strong breeze just as much as they could stagger under all sail. You may fancy they were cracking on when I tell you that a schooner had her boat, that was on the lee side deck comfortably floated out of her.

---

* So designated while escorting the Royal Yacht

There were 34 yachts at anchor off Cowes, and 12 or 14 off Ryde, nearly all under weigh yesterday. Every body says that they never saw such a muster of yachts before.

I should say the force of wind was about 7. A ship might have carried single reefed topsails and Top Gallant sails . . .

I have had a delicate little scratch with the 2nd Capt of the Yacht (Capt. Crispin (a beast)), and went to Denman. However he gave it against me, so I put it in a large new pipe which I smoked and washed down with a glass of grog, and after that returned to my normal state.

The *Sparrowhawk* came round from Plymouth in 13 hours, 135 miles.

We had a lot of rain the day before yesterday and yesterday up to noon when it cleared up. When the yachts started it was raining so hard and so thick that you could not see a ¼ of a mile.

You will see all the particulars of the race in the papers much better than I can give them as I did not know the names and only enjoyed it as a beautiful sight . . .

H.M. Yacht *Sparrowhawk*, fast to the coal Hulk, Plymouth Sound,
Tuesday August 11th, 1856

Dearest Parents,

Here I am again. Last night we anchored in Torbay, got under weigh at 8 this morning and were in here at 11.45, a distance of about 40 miles.

The Yacht going very easy walks by us as if we were at anchor.

The Queen has gone into the harbour to receive addresses &c. and the *Sparrowhawk* has gone along side the coal hulk in the sound to Receive coal!

I can't tell you anything of our further movements.

HMS *Sparrowhawk*, Plymouth Sound, Friday August 14th

My dear Father

I received your letter of the 12th yesterday.

In the first place I shall proceed to put your mind at rest as to the queries you start.

Firstly (as the parson says)

Pringle showed some want of knowledge of the service in sailing without me. Had anything happened to the ship on the way round it would have been disagreeable for me but he would have been turned out of the service as sure as fate.

I am quite sure his sailing without me was not through any ill feeling on his part, on the contrary, he thought that I would be able to start by train that night and would be at Portsmouth before the ship in the morning, and nobody would know anything about it.

In arriving at Portsmouth he did quite right in mentioning that I was left behind, as he naturally must have made sure that the Admiral would notice my not reporting the ship.

His great mistake was that after hanging on as long as he could in the Sound (which he did), when the Senior officer in the Sound made signals at him, instead of going, he should have made the signal 'Capt. is on shore'.

However he will know better another time.

Now for the particulars of the little scratch with Crispin.

A signal was made from the Yacht to us and to *Cormorant* for 1st Gigs. Now my 1st Gig is so valuable that she can't go anywhere without me in her.

So I went; Crispin informed me that he does not want me, but that he wants a four oared gig to attend on the Yacht, (I suppose to bring off pots, kettles, deputy nurse maids, assistants, band boxes &c &c).

So I told him that I had only my own 4 oared gig, and that I wanted her myself.

He told me I must send some boat.

I told him that if I did I should so weaken the ship's company that I should not be able to carry out Capt. Denman's orders into effect, and therefore I wished to see Capt. Denman.

I saw him and he gave it against me. I sent the 5 oared gig and put it in my pipe, as I told you before.

I dare say the schooner was not so near as the master made out, people always exagerate. I did not think of shuddering, as my philosophy came to my aid. A miss is as good as a mile.

What's done can't be helped. I am so sorry you should have been kept awake about me.

The Queen started this morning by rail as I expected yesterday, and the yacht sailed for Porstmouth, and we now return under the orders of the Admiral here.

Oh! How I do wish something would turn up to send me out of England.

With best love to the Mother and all.

FIVE

HMS *Surprise, 1857-1859*

To be ashore and unemployed as a junior officer was almost a condition of the peacetime service, while to be abroad and on the high seas, with the opportunities of bounty, distinction, and most vitally, promotion, was the ambition of all. After his 'inshore' service in 1856 in the Channel Fleet, Cresswell itched to be sent abroad again. As it happened, a notorious maritime incident in the Far East became the catalyst for his return to the waters he had known as an apprentice.

In October 1856, the lorcha *Arrow* out of Hong Kong was boarded while in the harbour of Canton by a Chinese officer and a squad of soldiers. Twelve crew members were carried off, and the British flag lowered by the boarding party. The crewmen were returned, but the diplomatic incident escalated to the point where it was decided to send reinforcements to the British fleet based in Hong Kong. In this case, the Prime Minister, Lord Palmerston, lived up to his 'send a gunboat' reputation. This was to be Cresswell's opportunity for service away from home, and in command of his own vessel.

In March 1857 Cresswell was appointed commander of HMS *Surprise*, dispatch vessel, for service in China. It was the answer to his plea the previous August: 'How I do wish that something would turn up to send me out of England.'

This second passage to China could hardly have been less like his voyage out in the sailing ship of the line HMS *Agincourt* as a volunteer fifteen years earlier. Now he was in command of a screw-propelled vessel, with auxiliary sail on two masts and a coal-fired steam engine. He sailed in company with fifteen other vessels, under his old friend Sherard Osborn, in HMS *Furious*. Cresswell in *Surprise* had charge of five ships, his own dispatch vessel and four gunboats.

As often in the Navy, getting started was no easy business. Having joined his ship in March, he was still chafing at the bit for orders in mid-April: 'I believe it is the wish of the Admiralty to crush any zeal that a Naval officer may have.' One cause of delay was the difficulty of assembling the flotilla of gunboats at Plymouth; and the prospect, even when launched was daunting: 'I have seen Osborn . . . He says he is to have 16 Gun boats under him, a nice little family, but a monstrous troublesome one.'

HMS *Surprise*, Plymouth Sound, May 1st, 1857

My dearest Parents

Our orders for sea came down yesterday, but as one of the Gun boats broke down on the way from the eastward and is now under repair, and also our having to wait for the *Hesper* (Store ship for the Squadron) not yet arrived, and nobody knowing where she is or what she is doing or anything about her; the exact time of our making a start must remain uncertain.

Osborn would like to be off as soon as today is over, it being Friday.

The order of sailing is as follows:

Furious (Osborn)

Hesper

Port Division		Starboard Division	
Surprise	Cmdr Cresswell	*Cormorant*	Lt Saumarez
Lee	Lt Graham	*Banterer*	Lt Pim
Janus	Lt Jones	*Watchful*	Lt Whitehead
Drake	Lt Arthur	*Woodcock*	Lt Pollard
Algerine	Lt Forbes	*Clown*	Lt Lee
Kestrel	Lt Rason	*Teaser*	Lt White

You will see by this that I am to bully the Port division, Saumarez, the Starboard, and Osborn the whole.

We got in 26 tons of coal yesterday, 5 in the stoke hold and 21 on deck, delightfully clean work.

HMS *Surprise*, at sea Lat 37.53 Long 11.52, May 12th

My dearest parents

We have spent the last 3 or four days collecting the gun boats, that always make a point of scattering at night.

We hardly ever can carry enough sail to steady the ship, we outsail every thing else so much. We spend most of our time with every thing furled rolling in the trough of the sea.

Madeira, May 16th

We got in this morning, only 2 of the gun boats not turned up. When I last wrote we had the *Watchful* in tow; last night the *Watchful* having recovered a little, and seeing another little chap astern apparently very sick, I went back for him, telling the others to make the best of their way.

Osborn is a great man, a philosopher. Speaking to him about the irregular proceedings of the Gun Bts he says 'Let them alone, and they'll come home and bring their tails behind them.'

While out riding with his fellow officers on shore at Madeira, Cresswell found an old friend: 'Capt' Cresswell?', 'Mrs Liddell!' Picnics and other plots were hatched, and Mrs Liddell was invited on board the *Surprise*. Mrs Liddell, and her husband, the Dean of Christ Church, Oxford, were the parents of Alice, heroine of Lewis Carrol's *Alice in Wonderland* and *Through the Looking Glass*, written five years later.

Cresswell put the ship's company to a good deal of trouble for the visit of Mrs Liddell, the Dean and other members of their party holidaying in Madeira.

May 19th

There is a lady coming on board to see me in the afternoon.

I believe the officers think I am a little cracked, I have been rousting about so, to make the ship smart, such a fuss about the gig's awning, and the gig's crew being in their very best, all the men being dressed clean in their white frocks and trousers, and oh such trouble to have a good accomodation ladder rigged to come up the side!

Parry,* who by the way has more devilment in him than enough, asked me this morning if I should be glad to leave Madeira. When I told him that I should, he looked as if he did not believe me.

---

* Lt. Charles Parry, son of Sir Edward and Lady Parry, close friend of Cresswell, and his second-in-command. Just as Cresswell had his chances at sea through 'interest', it is likely that he chose his friend Parry, and thus used his patronage to secure the place for him.

Oh dear, Oh dear. We are to sail at 8. My chief engineer is a fool. He can't see that there is any thing that would require a few days at anchor to put to rights in the engine room!

Well, you have got lots of nonsense so now goodbye.

The visit to Madeira lasted only three days since Osborn was anxious to press on with his squadron. Before leaving the island, Osborn issued two orders re-arranging the conduct of the flotilla:

HMS *Furious*, Madeira, May 18th, 1857

Memo,

With a view to forward H.M. Service I have taken upon me the responsibility of dividing the Squadron into four divisions.

Each division will without unneccessary expenditure of coal make their way to Rio according to the following proceedings.

1st: Sail down the NE Trades passing 5 to 8 miles to the West of San Antonio, one of the Cape de Verd* Islands.

2: On losing the NE Trade the senior ships of divisions will tow their division into the SE trade.

3: If possible and without tacking cross the Equator in 25 W. Long, and with judicious use of steam, proceed to Rio de Janeiro.

4: Coal and provision and await my arrival at that port.

As the utmost expedition is necessary to reach Hong Kong before the commencement of the Typhoon season I feel assured every effort will be made to push for our destination and officers will make every effort for that end.

Sherard Osborn, Capt.

To: Comm. Cresswell &c.

Memo No 2   *Furious*, Madeira

Further arrangement of Squadron will be as follows and the Commanders of the respective ships will immediately place themselves in communication with the senior officers of their division.

---

* Cape Verde Islands.

1st Division		2nd	
Furious	Osborn	*Cormorant*	Saumaurez
Janus	Jones	*Firm*	Nicholas
Drake	Arthur	*Banterer*	Pim
Lee	Graham	*Clown*	Lee

3rd		4th	
Surprise	Cresswell	*Algerine*	Forbes
Lee	Graham	*Kestrel*	Rason
Watchful	Whitehead	*Hesper*	
Woodcock	Pollard		

The Rendezvous are as follows:

1st   5 miles to the West of Cape St Antonio, Cape de Verd Isld.

2nd   Long 25° W on the Equator

3rd   Cape Frio

4th   Rio de Janeiro

It is desirable the engines be used as little as possible whilst running down the NE Trade and steam should never be got up without the sanction of the senior of the division unless to prevent parting company at night time; above all the high pressure engines should never be used at full speed in salt water.

       Signed

       S Osborn   Capt. & Senior Officer

The difficulties posed by Sherard Osborn's orders, that is to keep up to time, but not to burn up their supplies of coal, are illustrated in this letter home to his sister-in-law Charlotte Cresswell:

HMS *Surprise*, at sea Lat 31°57' Long 17°31', Thursday May 19th, 1857

My dear Charlie

I am very fidgety about my division of Gun boats. I have been on deck all day except when writing this letter.

Last night when I went to bed at 11.45 all the division of gun boats were close to me, when called this morning at daylight, one was reported not to be in sight. I had taken in the fore sail so as not to outsail them, and then in a fine night when I had I thought secured a few hours to forget gun boats, to be told one was out of sight, how it made me swear.

However the moment I went on deck I found the lost sheep, and as the weather has turned out most lovely, and there is a nice little fair breeze and all my gun boats are in company, and the awnings are nicely spread, and the men are all in white, and the scuttles are out and skylights open, in my cabin and all over the ship. The officers are all in nice straw hats, and my cabin is charmingly cool, and the steam is not up.

I dine in with the officers today in the Gun room. I always do on Thursdays. On Fridays and Saturday I give dinner parties. I ask three on each day, and can just set out my little table without putting a leaf in and we have very snug little parties I assure you.

May 26th

We make 50, 60, 70 or 80 miles a day generally with nothing but our Fore Topsail and Top Gallant sail set. We have to keep under very small sail to keep company with the Gun boats.*

I fear I am a very bad captain. I am too intimate with the officers.

The great crimes I have comitted are establishing a Whist club, which meets about 4 times a week, twice in my cabin and twice in the Gun room. Then I join the officers smoking, smoke a short black pipe, bathe with the ship's company, wear a white jacket on the Quarter deck, look after the cooling of my own claret &c.

June 2nd

The other day a poor fellow that I had taken onboard from the *Watchful* having fever died. I had the *Watchful* in tow at the time. The *Woodcock*, the other small gun boat of my division had got a long way ahead and the *Lee*, the large one was about 5 miles on the starboard bow.

At 9 in the morning the *Watchful* made the signal that she wanted medical assistance. I did not like to stop, the *Woodcock* was so far ahead that I was doubtful, with the very bad look out that is always kept in Gun boats, if she would heave to.

So I determined to hold on until 1.30 and then communicate with the *Watchful*, and I made the signal to her for any of her men that wished to attend the funeral at that time. At one I made the signal to the *Lee* and

---

* For a comparison with what *Surprise* could do, see below, 22 September 1857.

Woodcock to heave to, and enforced it with a gun. The *Lee* did so after having run on a mile or so, but the *Woodcock* went on. At 1.30 I hove to. The sick of the *Watchful* came on board, and while the doctor was fixing them, I had the funeral so that no time might be lost.

I bundled the *Watchful*s over the side, and made all sail, but notwithstanding this had caused us a detention of 45 minutes and the *Woodcock* was out of sight. However, I cracked on every possible thing. In about an hour I saw my runaway about 2 points on the port bow, but instead of being hove to waiting for us he was standing away on the port tack.

By 4 o'clock we had closed the *Woodcock* considerably. The *Lee* was about abeam and still standing on the port tack about 5½ miles off. I made her recall, and fired guns but all no go. As she was to windward now I hardly expected her to hear my guns, but if there had been any look out on us kept, she must have seen our signal.

At 9.30 when off the Rendezvous I fired two guns, one on each side and a rocket to show the division our position. Next morning at daylight both the *Lee* and the *Woodcock* were out of sight!

Sunday June 7th

We are not far from the Line. We lost the NE Trade yesterday. I immediately took both the gun boats in tow. You know I have lost the *Lee*, so only have 2 left now.

The heavy pull on us now is in the stoke-hold. How the men can live in it is wonderful to me in a temperature of 140°.

Lat 1°4'N Long 24°50'W, Wednesday June 10th

On Monday morning about six o'clock Parry (who always keeps the morning watch), called me to say that there was a gun boat steaming up astern. She came up with us. It was the *Firm* (Nicholas). That mad man Saumaurez whose division he was in had sent him in to buy bullocks at San Antonio. He got two at £7.10s a piece, miserable half-starved things, and as he did not fall in with his gallant commodore, he did not like to kill them, and they had been existing for some days on bread dust. We asked if they wanted anything or if we could do any thing for them.

Oh no, they were all right, and going on to the rendezvous on the line. This was at 6 AM. At 9 we observed her make sail, and saw no more smoke. When we came up to her, she had only broken down in all her boilers, and also wanted immediate medical assistance, a man having fever on board very bad.

I took the *Firm* in tow, and I cast off the other two and made them get their steam up. The next morning of the 11th, the *Watchful* broke down.

In the afternoon twigged a ship standing towards us. A boat came on board to report her. She was bound with coal from Leith towards Melbourne.

Here was a go, to coal in the middle of the Atlantic at night not 150 miles from the Equator, a good long swell and two gun boats in tow tickled my fancy. So to work we went with a will. We had to work the coal in the vessel, we had to work our two cutters and hoist it on board.

The men worked very well, it was tremendous work. We commenced at 7 and got about 19 tons in by 12.30. The *Firm* also got about 9 tons.

The next morning the gun boat that I had not in tow had quite broken down. There was also every sign of the SE trade setting in strong, so I determined to take them all in tow. I gave the *Firm* my stream chain besides my 10 inch hawser, from the *Firm* to the *Woodcock* my 7 inch hawser and a 5, from the *Woodcock* to the *Watchful* two 5 inch.

June 24th

The trade remains very light. I have about 30 tons of coal in the ship and shall, when within 250 miles of our port, get the steam up and make the gun boats do the same then, as they break down, take them in tow which I would bet 2 to one they both do before they have been steaming 24 hours. I know that the commanders of them will be as mad as hatters at this, as what they would like would be to be towed to just outside and then steam in. They would then probably say that they had steamed the greater part of the way out from England, and that if it had not been for my delaying them they would have been in Rio 3 weeks before.

Rio de Janeiro, July 3rd

Here we are. The *Lee* here all right. We arrived here the night before last and found all the good people in but one Gun boat who came in the next morning.

Have received no end of praise and am to be reported to the blockheads at the Admiralty as a very good boy.

Poor Saumaurez made a mess of it, ran away from his gun boats, no end of a shine about it . . .

HMS *Surprise*, Lat 34°10' Long 32°38', July 15th, 1857

My dearest Parents,

We anchored at one o'clock AM July 1st in Rio harbour. We made the entrance in the evening and steamed in; the town has recently been lighted with gas and it had a most beautiful effect entering the harbour.

The abolition of the slave trade is proving the ruin of the place combined with the dreadful mortality there was amongst the black population a short time ago with cholera. The consequence of these two causes is that labour is at an unnatural high price.

The dirty lazy scoundrels that coaled our ship, working only from 7 in the morning until 5 in the evening and going away for an hour to breakfast and two hours for dinner, and doing about half a man's work during the time they were actually at it, receive something over 7s 6d a day, only 6d short of a Commander's half pay.

I took my carpet bag onshore the day after our arrival proposing to have a comfortable night in a four-poster, but the rooms at the hotel were bad! Filthy in the extreme. I now was rather in a fix.

Just as I was in despair, my ship four miles off coaling the other side of the bay, who should I tumble across but my dear friend Chas Forbes. Chas had his gig onshore. His ship was over at the coal station.

We had a very fair dinner and then lighting our backeys, pulled over to our ships. It was a lovely moonlight night, and very delightful.

Cape Town, August 19th, 1857

My dearest parents

I lost all my Gun boats in our passage across from Rio. We had such dreadful weather.

Our experience of Gun boats quite goes to confirm the melancholy accounts of the dudness of them. It is quite heart-breaking.

I understand the French Gun boats in China are very far superior to ours and they are not always breaking down as they condense all the water required for the boilers so that the evaporation takes place from fresh instead of salt water so the tubes do not get foul.

The destination of the troops going to China was altered to India. The artillery, the Garrison of Cape Town have been taken by Sir William

Wiseman in the *Penelope*, and a volunteer corps was doing duty. I saw the Attorney General (who is a private) on sentry duty.

Sir George Gray, the Governor at the Cape, has taken the responsibility of altering the destination of the troops bound to China, and also sending troops from the colony. His very decisive and prompt measures may just possibly be the means of saving India.*

We sailed from Simon's Bay on the evening of the 25th of August, and steamed to the Southward until we got into about Latitude 36, then having a Southerly breeze I made sail on starboard tack and got the screw up. I fully expected to get Westerly winds when I got out of the local influence of the continent, however instead we got Easterly first, N.E. then S.E. then East although we went South into nearly 41° and blowing as if it would blow the eye teeth out of one.

One morning at 5 o'clock I was woke by the ship heeling over a good deal for her, for she is as stiff as a church, and rang my bell, but as it was not answered slipped on flannel trousers and jacket and went on deck.

I found Parry with rather more on his hands than is pleasant, the fore topsail in ribbons, the fore trysail throat halyards having carried away. That was all right but that a tremendous whole main trysail was set, the spanker was half scandalized, the wind roaring and howling like fury and the ship carrying the helm laid a-weather and ploughing along I am afraid to say how fast for I had something else to do than heave the log.

The first thing I did was to let go the main throat halyards; it is the only way to manage if caught in a heavy squall.

We now sent the Topmen aloft to try and save as much of the topsail as possible, but when about 14 men were in the top, to my horror I saw the foremast commence to work fearfully with the roll of the ship. Every roll it got worse. I think this was the most trying moment of my life. I felt it would only be by the mercy of providence if I got the men down before the foremast went.

The rigging was now so slack and every moment becoming more so that the lee side, or rather that side that we rolled to, hung in a perfect bite, and the opposite side the shrouds would be brought up with such a tremendous jerk that I thought they must go every moment, in the event of which we must have lost our watch of blue jackets and foremast, for the sea was now running very high, but by God's mercy I got all the men on deck, I really felt my foremast almost a secondary thing.

---

* A reference to the Indian Mutiny.

Two smart fellows got a gasket round the fore top-sail before they came down.

I was standing just in the gangway abreast the main mast. Parry was about 4 feet before me.

When a heavy sea strikes us it reminds me of a great big man striking a very small boy with his open hand. A big sea did strike us hard, all along the starboard waist.

I had only time to sing out hold on by your eyelids (a favourite position amongst sailors) when my breath was taken away from the fact that I was under water. There was a big crash at the same time. The moment the salt water was clear of my eyes I woke up to the fact that HMS *Surprise* was minus her starboard waist hammock nettings and I was very much afraid for her First Lieut, he being on the deck at my feet pale, and stunned.

The sea had hit the hammock nettings a clout, and the hammock nettings, backed by 30 or 40 tons of water hit Chas Parry a clout over the back. This was jolly. Every blessed thing on the deck washing about, our [?holds'] guns working in a most playful way not having had time to get the proper amount of securing for a gale of wind on, and the First Lt. in the Capt's arms.

The Master, who was making himself useful getting the spanker furled, I hailed together with a marine to take our used up First below and a boy to call the doctor.

Now to find out what was the matter with the fore rigging and if possible save the foremast. What do you think it was? I blush to write it, as although I was at Cape Town during the time the lower rigging was setting up I felt lowered in my own estimation in commanding a ship where such a thing could happen.

I found that the lanyards of the fore-rigging the starbord side had not been properly secured, without being hitched. I got them all secure, capstan bars in the rigging, not without some difficulty.

I then got the topsail furled and as soon as it was practicable, which was not till next morning, sent all my yards down from aloft, this of course relieved the mast greatly.

As soon as the weather moderated we set up lower rigging, and we had nearly to remake our fore topsail before we could send it aloft.

The following morning Parry was all right again, he had been stunned and was a little shaken by the blow.

I have now had some little experience in this ship in gales of wind for

14 days before arriving at the Cape and for 10 days after and she is by far the most beautiful sea boat I ever was in.

You must not understand from this that she keeps her decks dry. During the least sea the decks are wet. But as far as ease and I believe safety goes she could not be better.

We certainly have shipped two heavy seas, the one that knocked Parry a thump on the back and one shortly after leaving Rio and that, as far as I could make out, was one of those mountain waves that cruize about the mighty deep without rhyme or reason.

Some of my jolly tars assert that they heard this wave coming for some time before, although quietly seated on the lower deck getting their breakfast.

A ship 226 feet long, 26 feet broad and her deck only about 5 feet above the water must wash the decks now and then.

Our deck is almost always wet, in fact in anything approaching bad weather we all live in a state of pickle, and the Master of the *Surprise* has designated her not inappropriately, the half-tide rock.

We had a earthquake whilst at anchor in Simons Bay. It was felt strongly at Cape Town and all about the neighbourhood. All the merchant ships came in dock full of yarns about having experienced winds quite opposite to what experience had taught them to expect.

Some say that the expected Comet is having a lark with our little Earth, some that he is going to run us down. This troubles my head but little although getting foul winds is a great bore.

On the 6th of Sept we at last got a fair wind, since which time we have done very fairly.

September 22nd

I send you a list of a few of our times. Pretty fair work I think you will consider it:

Sept	7th	200	
	8th	120	
	9th	185	
	10th	186	
	11th	110	
	12th	114	
	13th	222	222
	14th	205	205
	15th	237	237

16th	196	*196*
17th	196	*196*
18th	207	*207*
19th	228	*228*
20th	128	*1491*
21st	196	*213* av. per day for 7 consecutive days
22nd	227	Ave per hour 8.875.
(16)		*2957*

184 average a day for 16 consecutive days.

Average per hour 7.7 knots for the 16 days.

Average per hour for the greatest run, the 15th of Sept. 9.8 knots.

Greatest logged for any hour 11.5.

The other morning we fell in with a large ship to the Southward of us, and as she was standing more to the Northward than us, we soon closed.

We found as she got near that she was full of troops, a very fine straight ship under all plain sail. She got ahead of us and on the starbord bow, her decks rigging, tops &c covered with soldiers, and a lot of ladies and officers &c on the poop. As she passed us they manned the rigging and cheered us, which of course we returned. In this respect they beat us having, I should think 700 pair of lungs against 90.

He now shot ahead about 200 yards, and for a few minutes we seemed to be going about equal, then it was evident we were gaining.

The excitement now was something tremendous. Two ships close together going 10 knots at least with a grand long sea is a fine sight. We were decidedly gaining. Now my fellows cheered again like mad men, the soldiers manned the rigging and I much doubt if that place ever heard such a row before.

We had made the signal: where are you bound? but as we were now within a stone's throw of him, the skipper called 'Calcutta!'. Now we gave them the very best cheer our lungs could produce, and in return held up a board with Canton in immense white letters. On this all the cheering burst out again.

By this time we had taken the wind out of his sails and shot ahead of him, however he soon got the wind again, and now it was fair sailing. Nevertheless we kept steadily gaining and soon were so far ahead that I put my helm up and ran across his bows and shaped my course. I had kept up to his for the fun, now the ensigns were again hoisted as we had been firing away with signals, and his was dipped three times.'

Again the men cheered, again the white handkerchiefs of the ladies waved. It being a thick day we both soon lost sight of one another on our different roads.

Straits of Borneo, October 5th

We arrived at Anyer at 9 pm on the 3rd, 39 days from the Cape. Osborn had left with all the squadron except the *Hesper* & *Janus* & *Clown* gun boats. He had first arrived at Java Head some weeks before us, had been to Singapore and also to Batavia.

I think I told you the orders we got at Rio from him were not to go to the Cape.

I wrote to Osborn by the *Banterer* officially giving my reasons for deviating from his orders. I expected that he would be savage, I should lose the character of good boy that I got for sticking to the gun boats between England and Rio.

However I have now received a letter of which the following is an extract:

'My dear Cresswell,

I have just time to say that I am perfectly satisfied with your reasons for visiting the Cape, and shall be very glad to see you, &c. &c.'

October 6th

Here we are at the old thing again, towing a gun boat, when about halfway through the Malay Straits one evening we come up with the *Banterer* at anchor, quite broken down. You remember that Pim commands her. I intended to have run all night, and should have been easily at Singapore today. But as it was I anchored, and took him in tow the next morning at day light.

Going on all night, 6 knots. I have decided to come to off the Strait tonight, and get under weigh at daylight tomorrow. I would try to make my passage through it at night, if it was not for Wright, who has heard rather bad news of his wife, and I think that makes him rather nervous, and he won't sleep properly whilst we are under weigh at night.

HMS *Surprise*, Hong Kong, November 14th

At last My dearest Parents

I am able to date my letter from Hong Kong, we, that is myself and two gun boats arrived here yesterday. I sailed with one gun boat to Moria, an island not far from Labuan.* At that place we fell in with the *Furious* again. There chanced to be a row about our Consul at Brunei, he having gone up some river on a cruise of pleasure. A report reached the Sultan of Brunei that he had been drowned.

The Sultan sent despatches to Moria, which I got hold of, one being for the Governor of Labuan. I took my gun boat over and found Osborn and the Governor. The next day we all went up to Brunei in a body to avenge the consul when much to our surprise we found the supposed dead man at his door to receive us. So we wound up the day by going to Court and chin-chinning the old Sultan. How odd it is the way events in one's life come round. It was about 12 years ago I was doing the same thing.

We are not sorry to be out I can assure you. Six months and 10 days on the passage.

I think as far as I can make out I stand well with the Admiral. I like his looks very much. The only thing I do not like is that the Flag Capt.† seems to have too much to do with things in general.

I dined last night with M'Clure.‡ If his wine was not bad, I drank too much of it, for I am as seedy as an owl today.

I have just received a letter from Sir Wm Seymour acknowledging my letter reporting proceedings 'I entirely approve . . .', so you see I get patted on the back by all hands.

This place is chock full of Men of war of all nations, English, French, Spanish, Dutch, American, Russian &c. I have just returned from a big American frigate where I have been paying my respects. She is wonderful, we must look out for those Stars and Stripes chaps.

We start for up the river next week, we do not hear anything of the state of preparation for us there.

HMS Surprise, Hong Kong, Nov 28th

My dear parents,

I must again put you off with a very short letter, but I am so seedy that I can hardly see out of my eyes, I have one of my delightful influenza colds.

---

* Island off NW Borneo
† Capt. Robert Hall, R.N.
‡ Cresswell's skipper in the *Investigator* in the Arctic, 1850–53.

Parry is quite well. All the Gun boats have now arrived, and Osborn is going up the river with Lord Elgin, which I am very glad of, as Lord E. will soon see what sort of a man he is and justice will be done him. There is a most paltry little jealousy, Capt. Hall being at the head of it, got up against Osborn.

HMS Surprise, Whampoa*, Just between Davis and Junk Islands,
December 3rd

My dearest Parents

We came up the river from Hong Kong last Friday six days ago as far as Tiger Island where the Admiral &c &c were at anchor. The Admiral inspected us and we had some shot practice at a target which was very good.

Shadwell and a lot more are at Macao fort. M'Clure is just above the second bar and there are other ships in other places distributed about. The Commodore, Hon. Charles Elliot is a very nice fellow. I understand although he has hardly ever done any body a bad turn, that he never will put out so much as his little finger to serve any one that is under him. This is not as it should be, and how different to Osborn. The absurd jealousy there is out here against Osborn is too bad.

I must give the Commodore credit for not joining in it, but it is a saying on board the Flag ship that a man that is a friend of Osborn can't be of Capt. Hall.

The squadron is very slack. How different it was under Sir Thomas Cochrane.

We, (that is to say we small people) hear nothing of what is going on at Canton, but the report is that they are not taking any steps to place the forts in an efficient state, what poor fools they must be for we are giving them every time and opportunity to do so.

I must consider myself as being very fortunate in being up the river, as before we arrived it was fixed that I should have gone up to Shanghai to relieve Dew, but Saumarez has made such as ass of himself on the passage out that the Admiral sent him to the North although senior to me.

This is an odd sort of war. Every ship with her bum boat, and the men get fresh beef and vegetables as regularly as if we were at anchor in Portsmouth harbour.

---

* Up river between Hong Kong and Canton.

December 4th

We black sheep had a very pleasant dinner last night with the Commodore. He was a Post Capt. at 21, the youngest that has been made since the good old times; if you remember Sir T. Cochrane was a Commander at 16½, and a Post Capt. at 18.

I walked to the top of Davis Island this morning to see the sun rise. We always go about armed and with some of the boats crew as body guard, not feeling inclined to be encaged, impaled &c &c for the special amusement of John Chinaman, we also have a little excitement in being in the spot where so many fire rafts and devil machines were sent down on the ships last year.

There is one thing that rather puts my pipe out, and that is that the only thing we can get to eat is fowls and tough beef, but possibly one might be worse off 100 miles up a river in an enemy country. Oh and there is another hardship, we are very short of soap.

December 12th

I have moved about a mile and a half higher up the river and am stopping boats all day and night. Last night they fired at the ship. I had just come on board from dining with the Commodore, 10.30. We twigged a boat sloping along inshore. I sent a boat after her, and no sooner had she shoved off than we got a shot just across our bows.

I understand that the *Times* reporter* is quite on Lord Elgin's staff. Whitehead had Lord E on his Gun boat for a day or two. The *Times* reporter was with him, dining at his table &c.

Every body out here prostrates them selves to him, I am sorry to say even our friend Osborn and Chas. Forbes among the number.

I believe the gentleman is or was a barrister who could not get a brief. I hope my uncle the Judge never wounded him.

One of my boats has just returned from stopping boats. From one she got 4 doz. teal. This will make a change from fowl and beef. The Commodore has a capital cook, and as I dine with him about every other day I hope not to starve just yet. My cook is so bad that I have not got any pluck up to ask the Commodore to dine with me yet.

---

* George Wingrove Cooke (1814-65), *Times* Special Correspondent in China 1857-8. His letters from China were published by Routledge as *China 1857-1858*, and ran to six editions.

HMS *Surprise*, off Canton, December 27th, 1857

My dearest Parents

I am in a state of most dreadfull savageness, so you must forgive a rather crusty letter.

The principal part of the land force will not land tomorrow, but the day following and will make for SE and NE gates and take the place by escalade.

We have issued no end of proclamations telling the people to hook it but the Manchus have also been telling the people to stop, and although it is evident that some have cleared off since we have been here, yet there are many remaining.

What makes me so savage is that I am not included in the landing force, nor yet is Dew who is anchored next in line to me. We are the senior Commanders so it is a great shame. In fact the whole thing is a Flag ship's pidgeon. The reason they give is that we are the only two available ships in case of a row at Hong Kong.

There has been a proclamation issued in Canton to the effect that every body is to provide himself with a flag and a drum and on the advance of the barbarians the drum is to beat and all are to be ready to fight to the death, and goes on to say 'How can the few prevail against the many, how can it be permitted that the central land of flowers should fall into the hands of the barbarians &c.'

Monday December 28th

11 AM We opened fire this morning at daylight. The Chinese did not return it. The town is fired in many places. You must excuse more as I must go to the mast head to direct the fire, as if I am not there my Chaps get so wild in firing as we can't see from the deck what we are firing at.

The bombardment will continue all night, the landing party I think about 6,000 strong land on the right of the town tonight and storm tomorrow morning.

HMS *Surprise*, off Canton, January 4th, 1858

My dearest parents

The last time I wrote was during the bombardment of Canton. This day last week, December 28th the landing force consisting of Blue Jackets, Marines and troops, about 5,000 bayonets in all effected a landing with little or no resistance on the East side the City and encamped for the night. The original plan was that we should discontinue the bombardment at 6 on the morning of the 29th, but it was altered during the night to 9 for us to knock off, and the storming of the walls was altered to 9 also.

Now it seems that the French were under a troublesome little fire from gingalls,* and under these circumstances made a rush although not much more than 7.45 o'clock, and of course when our chaps saw the French charging, they could not be kept in. The Chinese troops made a miserable resistance as soon as they were dislodged from their cover they acted on the principle that 'he who fights and runs away will live to fight another day'.

On the evening before the attack the enemy came out in some force to attack us, but were shortly driven behind those walls again – poor Capt. Bate of the *Actaeon* was killed the same evening. He left the cover of some houses on hills to reconnoitre the walls for the best places to storm, when he was shot through the side and killed dead on the spot.

After the allies had taken all the eastern wall, the English went on and took the forts behind the place, Gough Fort, City Hill &c.

The only real mistake that was made, and that was caused by the impetuosity of the French, was that the bombardment from the ships continued for more than an hour after our forces had entered the town, but I understand that but few casualties are supposed to have occurred from it.

Our loss, I understand, in killed and wounded is about 120 or 130.

Amongst the former poor Bate and a poor little Midshipman.† Among the latter Lieut. Lord Gilford, a marine officer.

Bate is an irreparable loss. He was out here for many years before, surveying, and he had now come out to go to Japan in the *Actaeon*, but was stopped in his way by the Admiral for the Canton pidgeon. His talents and local knowledge have been immensely useful in this river.

I was sent down to Hong Kong with a hospital ship full of wounded, and was in time to attend the funeral.

The body had been sent to Hong Kong in the *Dove* Gun boat. At 3 in the afternoon all the boats assembled near the *Dove*, and formed two lines, and as there were several foreign men of war at Hong Kong, nearly

---

* A light swivel gun or heavy musket much used in China.

† Midshipman Henry Thompson.

all their officers and boats attended. The afternoon was lovely, the magnificent bay like a polished mirror, all the ships in the harbour had their flags half mast.

The *Tribune*'s barge had her band on board, and towed a cutter with the body, the coffin raised well above the gunwale and the sailors pall (the Union Jack) drooping gracefully over the coffin and boat. Then another cutter with the remains of the poor little Midshipman. As they left the *Dove* the *Tribune* commenced firing minute guns, the barge and cutter passed down between the two lines of boats pulling very slowly, the band playing the Dead March in Saul, only disturbed every now and again by the roar of the minute gun that would echo for a few seconds and remind one that the profession of him we mourned was that of arms.

And then again the music would swell, touching the very chords of the heart.

All the troops and marines were fallen in to receive and join the procession on shore. The Bishop read the funeral service, the volleys were fired over the grave, and we looked into the narrow home of the gallant fellow that four days before had been on board my ship full of health and vigour.

But to return to Canton, which I did the next day with my hospital ship. All was as when I left. The day that I was away Lord Elgin, (who has his headquarters abord the *Furious* about three miles from Canton a little way above the barrier) landed and marched round part of the town, and there had a grand turn-out, salutes, &c. &c.

There is a report that before he attacked the place the Chinese offered $6,000,000 to buy us off, but there are such a lot of yarns and stories flying about that you do not know what to believe, you constantly hear people saying they long to get the *Times* from England to find out what we are doing.

Hong Kong, January 8th

I am ordered up to Amoy immediately. We sail this afternoon. Jenkins of the *Comus* now at Amoy, and one of the senior Commanders out here has got the death vacancy. He is a good little fellow is white headed Bob, and I am glad of it.

Great news from Canton, Yeh, the Tartar General, and a lot more nobs have been taken.

HMS *Surprise*, Ning Po, March 18th, 1858

My dear parents

I have so much to say that I hardly know what to commence upon as I have to write to the Admiral a description of the harbours of Kilon and China Bay in Formosa, where I have been in this ship partly to obtain coal and partly to report on the coal obtained and the facilities for Men of War to procure it. I also expect Osborn on board any moment, to go for a walk.

I was relieved by the *Sampson* at Amoy on the 27th Feb. We left Amoy on the 1st. I had a Mr Taite on board, he is the first merchant of Amoy. He was rather seedy and wanted a cruise. He is a perfect merchant prince. From Amoy we went to Kilon on the NE coast of Formosa for the purpose above named. We arrived on the 2nd. Mr Taite was of the greatest use to me as an interpreter. We found that getting coal from the shore in any quantities in a short time was impracticable as there was not sufficient demand to make it worth while for any of the inhabitants to keep a depot.

The result is that if a junk should come in requiring a cargo she may have months to wait before she is laden, and often does so. Of course we could not wait, so I bought up a junk's cargo that she had been 7 or 8 month collecting.

HMS *Surprise*, Ning Po, April 30th, 1858

My very dear parents

I must give you an account of an excursion we made into the country. Ning Po is situated in a large alluvial plain surrounded by mountainous country, about 9 miles as the crow flies from the sea and 15 miles from the base of the hills inland.

Our object was to reach the high land furthest from Ning Po, and although I do not think it was more than 15 miles in a straight line, it must have been 30 by following the course of the river. Meadows, the British Consul at Ning Po, and Mr Justice Buller, a judge from Calcutta staying with the Consul, dined with me, and after dining we made our start in 5 boats. My boat was about 30 feet long, 6 broad with a cabin covered in about 12 feet long with a low table and stools and a nice bed place &c. The other boats the same except the Consul's, and his boat was built after his own plan and had a cabin about 12 feet by 7, and 6 high. This boat was the mess room, and Meadows' sleeping cabin. Then the

Judge and myself had two others of the five, the servants another and cooking another.

We had a strong tide with us and the following morning soon after daylight we found ourselves as far as our boats could take us. We now got cooleys, 16 in number to take our traps and mountain chairs for ourselves. We had about 9 miles of flat travelling and then 5 or 6 of hills. Each person has to take a relief of chair bearers, so with servants, cooleys, bearers, ourselves &c it swelled the party to nearly 40 people.

The travelling in chairs is pleasant. The Judge growled at it, but notwithstanding would not get out and walk. On arriving at the hills we all walked, and by the time we arrived at our destination, a Buddhist Temple where we proposed to take up our quarters, at one o'clock, having been up from 5, and only had a cup of tea before starting, we were quite ready for our chow.

There is some really fine scenery about this part of China. There are three waterfalls within walking distance of the temple, the most easterly about 7 miles from it. Getting up at 5 we started off for it one fine morning. The land about this fall is nearly 2,000 feet above the sea, with a very fine view into richly cultivated plains, and glorious hills and mountain sides. Meadows and myself went down into the valley of the fall; the Judge was not quite game for it.

We had a tremendous climb to get out, and it was a very hot day, so that we were not sorry to see the table laid for breakfast in a pretty little joss house. The Judge made a scandalous assertion that Meadows and myself polished off a bottle of beer and a bottle of porter each at that memorable breakfast. Fortunately I was able to retaliate on him for having made a very large hole in a bottle of claret, and he had not the excuse of having climbed about 700 feet of nearly perpendicular rock, and so we passed our time laughing and chaffing, yarning and smoking, eating and drinking.

We got up at 5 when I went to the nearest mountain stream to bathe, then a cup of tea and toast, then away on some excursion, taking our breakfast with us, not a piece of bread in one's pocket, but 7 or 8 cooleys with a table, chairs, cooking utensils, lots of eatables and drinkables &c &c.

The homeward journey, we did by foot and raft. After descending from the very high land, about 3 hours walking from the temple, we got to a town past which runs a mountain stream or river. The river is navigated by bamboo rafts, it being much too shallow for boats. From the extreme buoyancy of bamboo these rafts draw but very little water. They can always go with an inch or two, as the men get off and push them along.

The following day in the afternoon we got to Ning Po after 5 as pleasant days as I ever spent in my life.

You will have heard that Lord Elgin, the Admiral, and all the Ambassadors have gone north. You may fancy we do not like being stuck here, but I do not think we shall loose any thing by it in the long run, as I should not think any operations could be undertaken against Peking without a much stronger land force than we could muster at present, unless we give up Canton which would never do.

Sunday May 9th

I have just received orders to proceed immediately to the rendezvous off the Peiho.*

Good bye God bless you my dearest parents. If I do get a go in at em, won't I just.

HMS *Surprise*, Ning Po, June 2nd, 1858

My very dear parents

I arrived off Peiho, the rendezvous, on the 14th of May at 6 A.M. I went on board the Flag ship. The Admiral was not dressed, but Capt. Hall gave me to understand that I should go across the bar that or the next day. (It was past the highest springs when I arrived. I might have crossed without taking an ounce out of the ship, that or the next day.)

At 7, signal to *Surprise*: Admiral requests pleasure to breakfast at 8.

At 8 went on board Flag ship. Admiral on Poop. I very soon saw that all was wrong after a good deal of humming and hawing he gave me to understand I must go to the *Hesper*, complete coal, and go back to Ning Po. He certainly gave me the impression that he was very sorry to send me back, constantly said there would be nothing done to the north, I would lose nothing by it, assured me that he wished to serve every body but me in particular.

I was determined to give him a bit of my mind. I pointed out to him about 4 Commanders junior to me being made up for Canton, and to end all I told him I considered the *Cruiser* was the vessel that should be

---

* Peiho river, east of Peking.

sent to Ning Po. He asked me why? I told him for several reasons. 1st my vessel could go over the bar, and the *Cruiser* could not. 2nd Fellows, who was much my junior as a commander was promoted, and I was not, however it was no go 'he could not alter arrangements now &c.' So on board I went to convey this welcome news to my officers and men. You should have seen how pleased we all looked.

The *Hesper* was about 4 miles inshore of us full of coal. As I passed the *Furious* I dropped onboard in my gig and left the ship to go on. You may fancy the hearty reception old Osborn gave me. Lord Elgin was on deck and was very cordial. I could not resist telling him my troubles.

When I had finished he stamped his foot on the deck, and with rather a strong expression walked below.

That afternoon I know he sent a letter to the Admiral requesting him not to send the ship away. These words were in it: I earnestly request you will not send the *Surprise* away at this time when her services in the river would be of great importance. This I do not wish repeated in high quarters, as I was told it by one of the staff. Subsequently Lord Elgin told me he had done all in his power to keep the ship.

On my return to the ship I found we had been ordered to cease coaling and anchor near the *Hesper*. I naturally concluded that the Admiral had altered his mind, and we were to go over the bar.

There followed twenty-four hours of confusion, including another interview with the Admiral when Cresswell was once more ordered to complete coaling and prepare to leave. However, during the afternoon of the 18th, Capt. Hall reappeared at the *Surprise* with orders to prepare the ship's boats for a landing. By this time the spring tides of previous days had diminished to neap tides so that at high water *Surprise* and the large other ships could not have got over the bar at the mouth of the Peiho river.

The next day, the 19th in the afternoon the force was towed in by gun boats, Sir F Nicolson, Capt. Osborn and myself: *Pique, Furious, Surprise* composed the 1st Division, our two Gun boats were the *Staunch* and the *Bustard*. They took all our boats in tow. I had with me two 10-oared cutters, and my 5-oared gig and Whalers, a force of 6 in all. & Officers,

Parry, Patten, Gilbert, King and Master Bagge,* & Mr Buchan, engineer, 14 marines, 43 seamen.

That night I was fortunate to have my men told off for the *Nimrod*, where they were very comfortable. We, that is Sir F Nicholson, Osborn, Dew, some of Lord Elgin's staff dined on board the *Nimrod*. Dew gave us a very good dinner and we had a pleasant evening talking over the propects of the morrow. I must say I thought it more than doubtful if we should all meet again at that time next day.

The order of the day as far as I can make out was as follows: The *Cormorant* and *Nimrod* were to take up position, and engage the *Cormorant* the North, the *Nimrod* the South forts. Our gun boats with boats containing the 1st and 2nd Divisions to remain in position until the French and English Admirals had passed in Gun boat *Slaney*, and then to follow *Slaney* and land landing parties 1st Division on the North side of the river a little above *Cormorant*, 2nd Division about opposite on South. First Division to storm Forts on north shore, the Second division to take South forts in rear.

At 6 o'clock on the morning of the 20th May, 1858 a flag of truce was taken in from the Admirals by the English and French Flag captains demanding the surrender of all the forts, and giving them 2 hours to return an answer. The time was hardly up when the *Cormorant* began to advance.

The moment the Chinese saw this, they opened fire, which she did not return as the orders were to wait for the signal from the Admiral to engage, and the *Cormorant* had taken up her position off No 1 North fort before it was hoisted.

The enemy had all of their heavy guns on the East face of No 1 north fort, so the *Cormorant* got beyond the training of these heavy guns and only had to contend against small guns. She was so close that her grape and canister did good work.

The *Nimrod* was also by this time hard at work, and more beautiful practice than she made I have never seen.

The gun boats towing the landing divisions were not to advance until the Admirals in the *Slaney* had passed. Now the old Admirals did not seem to be in any mighty hurry to advance, and as they were out of range, and we were at anchor well within range with all our boats astern perfectly exposed you may fancy we were not a little glad at last to see

---

* Alfred Bagge, Midshipman and young friend of Cresswell's.

the *Slaney* with the two Admirals' flags side by side at the mizzen slowly advancing. As soon as the Admirals passed we weighed and followed.

The Chinese were still keeping up a very heavy fire. If it had not been for their strangely high firing, we must have suffered heavily. Some say they had their guns laid for high water, and that the water having fallen about 5 feet was the cause. Any how 20 shot went over us for one that fell short.

The 1st division was to land abreast of the first north fort. As soon as we got abreast the fort, Master Osborn being anxious to get into his gig astern, and my gig being before his, he ordered my gig to haul up that he might pass over her. There were several large boom boats towing astern of the gun boat, and projecting on each quarter. In the hurry, and the gun boat again going ahead full speed my gig swung across the bows of the boats just as I dropped into her. She filled and upset in 2 seconds.

Fortunately all the men jumped into other boats. I was not so fortunate, but got hold of the towing hawser of one of the big boats, went hand over hand along it until I came to the bow of her, where the men hauled me in. I had on at the time a heavy sword, a revolver, ammunition, a haversack &c. I fear I should have made but a poor fist of swimming under the circumstances if I had let go. As it was I got no more than being wet up to the middle.

The poor old gig went floating away bottom up, and the next gun boat took her amidships and finished her off. As the pieces went drifting out past the ships off the mouth of the river, and they made out the badge of the *Surprise*, there was a little speculation what Lieut. would get the Commander's vacancy.

We formed on the shore, and charged at our fort. Those of the Enemy that had not run before, ran now fast enough. A few were shot down by our rifles. We found a few dead, not so many as might have been expected from the way the place was riddled by Jack Saumarez' grape and canister. People say numbers were carried away before we landed. I think this very likely as the Chinese have a wonderful respect for the dead.

We now, after I think much too long a delay, advanced on further encampments. The Gun boats of our division, the *Staunch* and *Opossum* supporting us by water. I must diverge a moment to tell you the French gun boats were ordered to advance some minutes before ours, but notwithstanding ours were under weigh and advancing long first. There was rather a severe loss in the gun boats advancing up this reach, odd to say much more heavy in the French than English gun boats although they were so much after ours.

Shortly after we commenced our march I observed a place looking for all the world like a earthwork with a lot of flags on it. I pointed it out to Sir F Nicolson and he sent us to capture the work. I had half a hope that it might give us some fun, and it is a great thing to have the fun to oneself, and away we went at the double, myself 150 yards in advance of the skirmishers, and the skirmishers 200 in advance of the main party. You must remember my whole army consisted of about 45, my marines being employed as skirmishers, with the marines of the *Pique* and *Furious* ahead of the main body. However this earth work turned out what it was intended to be, a sell. It was nothing but a mud bank on which the Chinese had stuck a lot of flags with the idea that it would increase our idea of their defences, and to deter us from making an attack. It appears they were very nearly successful in this.

I was now anxious to join the division before they could get to the further targets. We had to foot for it but only just got up in time to join in the storming.

The Chinese made but a slight resistance and cut and ran. This proved to be a large encampment judging from the tents, I should say for 5 or 6 thousand troops, there were 5 or 6 brass guns of a very heavy calibre.

There was not a single man touched in our division after landing, and I believe the 2nd division was as fortunate as ourselves, with the exception of the French who succeeded in blowing themselves up with a Chinese magazine. The *Nimrod* now made her way up, and after spiking and capsizing the guns, and destroying the camp, we went on board and went as far up the river as a joss House on the left bank. The two gun boats of our division with this closed the days work. We had taken all the forts and about 280 guns with a loss on our side of 5 or 6 killed, and 16 wounded. The French had a much larger loss, 4 officers killed.

I believe the casualties of the Allies amount to 60, rather heavy if you consider that the number engaged did not amount to more than 1,600. The loss on the part of the enemy is hard to estimate. They say that the number killed found in the different forts amounted to 100.

The next day I was ordered to return to my ship. I saw the Admiral on board the *Coromandel* before I went out. He thanked me, and I have the following from him in writing:

'I beg you will accept yourself, and convey to your officers and men my thanks for and approval of the services rendered during the operations of yesterday which I shall have pleasure in mentioning to the Lords Commissioners of the Admiralty.

'Given under my hand &c.

'M. Seymour'.

I went on board the *Furious* before I sailed, and had a long chat with Lord Elgin. He was very much put out at my being sent away, was most kind to me, expressed himself much pleased that I should have been in for the fight of the 20th.

We sailed the same evening, arrived here the 25th.

June 10th

No more news since I was last writing, except a report that 20 missionaries have been murdered at Peking, many of them French and that France has declared war against China. I do not believe it.

HMS *Surprise*, Ning Po, June 30th, 1858

My very dear parents

I have been making excursions lately. A gentleman by the name of Ince came down from Shanghai and we made a party to go up to a celebrated temple about 20 miles in the country.

The temple of Tien Tsing is very celebrated. It, with its out-houses, courts and other buildings covers several acres. It is situated about 400 feet above the level of the Ning Po plain, fine hills rise on all side of it, covered with wood, chiefly pine and the graceful bamboo. There are now about 70 priests there, they perform service every day, in the principle temple, a building I should say about 90 to 100 feet long, and 80 or so broad, 70 high, with immense Josses in it, many of them 30 feet high, gilt all over. It is a great resort of pilgrims, many hundreds at a time.

Shortly after our return from Tien Tsing, Bro. Ince got up a party to go in his beautiful boat to Pootoo, an island situated outside China. This island is entirely given over to the Buddhist priests and temples. It is very beautiful, quite a gem on the sea.

We passed two days very pleasantly lounging about the island. One morning we walked to the top of the highest hill on the island before breakfast, and precious sharp we were when we returned after a 5 hours tramp, quite ready after a delicious swim for our breakfast consisting of fresh caught fish, curry, &c. &c. and iced claret and water.

We went over to Chusan after we had done Pootoo. How different it was to what I remembered it in the old *Agincourt*. Then there were several men of war in the harbour, two regiments on shore.

I went to the old places, there was the hospital from which many of our fellows had gone to their long rest, the map room of the officers where I had been to many a roaring dinner &c. &c. All deserted or inhabited by a few squalid Chinese and pigs.

After 4½ days we returned. I have now taken up my abode with one of the merchants of the place. His wife has got a young baby that kicks up a most abominable row. Oh what a mercy it is to know that if one ever does get home it will not be to a house full of squalling children. If it was not for this wretch of a child I should be very comfortable as it a cool house fronting, and about 6 yards from, the river, and my ship moored close off the house. When she swings her stern comes within about 8 yards of the shore.

HMS Surprise, Ning Po, July 20th, 1858

My dearest parents

I really have very little to write about unless it is to expostulate on the heat of the weather, which is perfectly awful. I never had such a broiling, or felt so much shut up in any previous voyage to the hot parts of the world.

You of course will have heard of the Treaty* being signed. I can't help feeling that Lord Elgin should himself have gone to Pekin.

HMS Surprise, Ning Po, July 31st

My dearest parents

I am ordered to the Cape. I expect the *Nimrod* down here from Shanghai every hour to relieve me. I go to Hong Kong to coal &c.

Master Osborn pays you a fine compliment dear mother. He says, talking about my promotion, 'In Mrs Cresswell's force and energy of character however I have great faith and she at any rate will not I am sure sit down and see you subjected to a gross injustice. If any letter from me saying how much I am indebted to you for assistance, and strongly expressing my astonishment at the manner in which you have been

---

* The Treaty of Tientsin, 27 June 27 1858, granting, among more than 50 clauses, wide right of access to Chinese territory.

passed over will be of any service, pray drop a line to say so'. Osborn is something like a friend, but I shall not make use of his noble offer until I hear of the promotions for the Peiho and the end of the war.

The uncertainty, waiting for news of his promotion to Captain, was to last a little longer yet, and was complicated by the time it could take for news to reach the fleet from the Admiralty. The decision to appoint him Captain was taken in London in September, but did not reach the *Surprise* until late in October. Cresswell continued to worry and fret about promotion for weeks after the decision had been taken at home.

But meanwhile he was not idle, and was chosen by Admiral Seymour to take part in a raid against pirates operating on the doorstep of Hong Kong. At the end of August he wrote home giving his account of the affair as reported to Admiral Seymour.

HMS *Surprise*, in a mud dock at Whampoa, August 31st, 1958
My very dear parents

In the first place I send you a copy of the despatch I wrote to the Admiral reporting my operations against the pirates and one of his reply:

To: H.E. Rear-Admiral Sir M. Seymour, KCB

Sir, I have the honour to inform you that, in compliance with instructions received from you on the night of the 22nd inst., directing me to proceed in search of piratical junks near the Leman Islands, and effect their capture or destruction, I proceeded to sea at daylight the following morning, having with me the launch and barge of Her Majesty's ship *Cambrian*.

Shortly after opening out from Hong Kong Bay the pilot pointed out three boats working to windward, and informed me that they were part of the piratical fleet. I fortunately at this time observed many masts in a small bay in the north-west part of the island of Ling-Sing, and being informed it was the main body of the piratical force I proceeded towards them.

Within about 1,700 yards they opened fire on me which I did not return until within about 1,000, when we engaged them with one port broadside, firing shot and shell.

I then directed the *Cambrian*'s boom boats to take up a position in shore of us, so as to be able to advance, taking them in the flank as their guns came within range. The enemy directed much of their fire to the boats, which was admirably replied to by Lieutenant J. W. Webb, as he steadily advanced with his boats.

The enemy opened on us at 8 a.m., keeping up a smart and well-directed fire with round shot and spear-headed rockets, and, as we closed, with grape and canister, and had we not kept on a continual move would doubtless have caused us material damage.

After about 35 minutes their fire considerably slackened, and at about 9 o'clock two of their largest lorchas blew up with a tremendous explosion, caused apparently by the bursting of one of our shells; they appeared immediately paralyzed, and their firing ceased. Taking advantage of this, I pushed on with my own boats, and, joining with the *Cambrian*'s boats, effected a landing within a very short distance of the junks, having observed the crews desert their vessels and take to the hills.

On advancing to the top of a neighbouring ridge some more piratical vessels were discovered in a snug creek in the opposite side, crowded with men and evidently prepared for an attack from seaward; our position completely commanded them, and by opening fire on them with our rifles, killing a great number, caused the others to run away, after a vain attempt to reach us with their gingalls, our height being to great for any effective fire from the large guns.

Not deeming it prudent to expose the men unnecessarily to the scorching heat of the sun, I ordered their return to the boats in preference to advancing by land, and returning myself to the *Surprise*, closed, and taking the boats in tow, steamed round abreast the creek, and fired a few shells. I then despatched the *Cambrian*'s and our own boats, under cover of our fire, to effect the capture of the junks. No resistance was offered, beyond the occasional firing of gingalls from the neighbouring hills, the junks being deserted.

Several of them being aground, and many others much shattered from our fire, we only succeeded in bringing out seven, so I ordered the remainder to be destroyed by fire.

On boarding and landing to effect this we found a number of dead Chinamen, and observed for the first time several guns mounted on shore, commanding the creek, which were destroyed.

The capture of the piratical fleet being completed, 19 having been set fire to and seven taken possession of, and observing the total destruction of the ones fired by the explosions of their several magazines, I proceeded on my return to Hong Kong, taking four of the junks in tow, the three others being in charge of officers with orders to follow, and arrived at this port at 9.30 p.m. with the four junks, the others arriving during the night.

Of the seven vessels we have in our possession, two are lorcha built, one mounting 28 guns, the other 24, from 6 to 24-pounders; the remaining ones being junks of from 7 to 16 guns.

Of those destroyed, five were heavily armed lorchas, the remainder averaging the same armament as above; in all mounting on board and on shore 327 guns, 103 of which are on board the vessels brought in.

I have great pleasure in bringing to you notice the conduct of Lieutenant J. W. Webb, of Her Majesty's ship *Cambrian*, for the very gallant and judicious manner in which he fought the boats of that vessel; and the assistance rendered me both on board and on shore by Lieutenant Charles Parry, Senior Lieutenant of the *Surprise*, as also the steadiness and zeal displayed by the other officers and men under my command.

The only casualty was Mr Mallet, mate of the *Cambrian*, who, I regret to say, was severly burnt from an explosion while firing one of the junks.

I have, &c.

S. Gurney Cresswell.

From: Sir M. Seymour, in reply:

HMS *Calcutta*, Hong Kong, August 25th, 1858

Sir, I have to acknowledge the receipt of your letter of yesterday's date reporting the successful result of your cruize after the Pirates, having captured & destroyed 26 vessels at the Island of Ling Ting, and I have to express to you my very high approval of your proceedings on this important service, which I shall bring to the favourable notice of the Lords Commissioners of the Admiralty.

You will convey the same to your officers and ship's company.

I am sir,

Your most obedient servant,

W Seymour,

Rear Admiral and Commander in Chief.

I have reason to believe he will bring my claims strongly before the Admiralty, as I think the old gentleman really wishes to serve me a good turn before my leaving the station. His selecting me out of many to go out after the pirates looks like it, does it not?

After the capture of the junks I arrived at H. K. at 10 PM and anchored near the *Calcutta*. I went on board. I was made much of and my dear friend Mr Ale was so delighted he would persist in continually shaking my hand.

Since I left England 16 months ago I shall have been 4 times brought before the notice of the Admiralty, three out of the four times for meritorious service in action, and the other time for the assistance I rendered in bringing the gun boats out, a most difficult, arduous and harassing duty.

I possess the complimentary thanks of the Commander in Chief on two occasions when engaged against the enemy, also a highly flattering private autograph letter from him expressing his acknowledgements for the zealous readiness with which I have at all times performed the duties assigned me, and particularly in the engagement at the mouth of the Peiho river.

September 5th

We have returned from Whampoa. Our valves were a little adrift, our keel was a little rubbed in places, which a few sheets of copper put all to rights. I expected to have found the bottom more bumped about than it was.

The way one is docked there is odd. There are no dock gates or caissons, but instead you are built in. As soon as the tide is low, the Chinese set to work and in quarter of no time there are two lines of bricks driven across the stern, these are lined with plank and mud thrown in between. It is wonderful how quick they raise this barrier, a few hours does it.

Then comes the pumping of the dock, which is done with irrigating machines. They are very common in China, on the same principle as a chain pump. This takes rather a long time and you have to put up with the clatter clatter for two days and nights.

We were 5 days in this mud dock in very hot weather, but I am thankful to say suffered but little in health. Some of the ships have had two thirds of their Ship's Co. knocked over. The Medical Inspector told me that from one of the gun boats 26 men would have to be invalided from the effects of it. He also said that one year in this climate takes more out of one than 5 in any other. From this station we invalided about 100 men a month beside those that die.

September 9th

We are all most savage here at a very violent leading article in the *Times* of the 19th of July against the Admiral. I call it an infamous distortion of facts and consider the man that wrote it is no Englishman at heart.

I dined with the Admiral last night. He is most kind in every way. He speaks most confidently of my finding my promotion at the Cape, but during my course through life I have had too many disappointments to believe in promotion until I have my commission in my hands.

Capt. Hall said to me last night 'Why you surely must have interest enough to get your step for the Peiho'. You see we always consider for an officer of fair standing if mentioned in despatches for any service, a little interest at the right time will do the business for him.

The despatches of my pirate affair will go home by this mail, and if I have not been made for the Peiho, it will give you a third chance of pushing for it. Do not forget the way I was slighted for Canton, my seniority and this being my second command.

I can now count my white hairs by tens. When I left I could count them by ones.

HMS *Surprise*, Singapore, October 26th, 1858

My very dear parents

Here we are, on our way to the Cape and the West Coast of Africa.

We were ordered to visit Borneo on our way to Singapore. We had a very long passage as the Southerly monsoon was strong, and I found nearly all my coal out when we were about half way. I went into two harbours on the coast of Cochin China when it was blowing hard from the South, however we managed to get to Labuan on the 28th. We had fever in the ship after leaving Hong Kong, 24 in the list at one time, a large proportion out of 90.

Possibly you can remember my Chief Engineer, Mr Purchase. He died at Labuan. A most respected man, however poor fellow, he had not sufficient control over his liking for drink. We found out since, he got a case of gin on board before we left Hong Kong and he drank himself into a state of Delirium tremens. I had not the least idea he was drinking to excess until 2 days before his death. He leaves a wife and children.

I took my ship up to Brunei and paid a visit to my old friend the Sultan. (The present Sultan is not the Sultan that we visited in the *Agincourt* in '44 and kicked out in '45). I then returned to Labuan and remained some days.

Penang, November 3rd

The mail up to the 26th Sept. arrived the day we left Singapore and in the home news I saw my promotion extract from the *Gazette*, and although I have searched all the other papers I can't find anything about it. I think it must be true as Leckie, Lieut Bland, Carter &c are with me and they are just the promotions that might be expected for the Peiho action.

I expect to be at least 7 weeks to the Cape. I believe there are steamers run now between the Cape and England, but do not know the times of their starting. So far as I can judge you may expect me about the middle of February.

HMS *Surprise*, Port Lewis, Mauritius, November 29th, 1858

My dearest Parents

I have seen the Navy list of October, and my promotion seniority 17th Sept.

There is one thing that is morally certain, and that is that if there is not a war or a kick up of some sort, there is but very small chance of employment for me for 2 or 3 years; Shadwell, Waynwright and men who are considered 1st raters have had to wait, it is but fair that seniors should be served first.

You will see if you look in the Navy list that in the last 110 Captains on the list, there are only 8 employed.

You will also see that out of 356 Active Post Captains, 88 are employed, not quite one 4th, so you can calculate my chance of employment. I am not growling mind, I merely wish to point out to you exactly how things stand.

Now about my rooms. Have you had new carpets by this time? If you have not the old ones must be nearly done for, and also the papers. All the three rooms should have the same carpet and paper, small patterns for small rooms, the paper should not be of too bright a pattern on account of the prints. Nothing could be nicer than the old paper, but if I remember right you said you could not get another border the same. Well I must leave it all to you, I can quite trust your taste.

November 30th

We sail tomorrow morning. Love to all at home and any near ones you may write to.

Good bye and God bless and keep you,

Your most loving son,
S. Gurney Cresswell.

SIX

Epilogue: HMS Scylla

From the spring of 1859 until September 1863, Cresswell suffered enforced idleness as a Captain on half-pay, exactly as he had predicted in his last letter from Mauritius in November 1858. His life was divided between London, the family home at Lynn, and his cousins in Northumberland. His letters reflect the interests of a young man enjoying mid-nineteenth century life in town and country. Once or twice at sea he had written of the pleasures he anticipated from home life. These dreams came, however, towards the end of the longer voyages – after four years at sea as a volunteer, or, understandably enough, after two and a half years in the Arctic.

He was not poor. Though one of a large family, he had his half-pay and more than £200 a year, and the banking business of the Gurney and Cresswell families was sufficient to allow him to persevere with hunting, to enjoy visits to the theatre in London, and to pursue the pleasures of travel and boating with the family. All the same, the enforced separation from his life's work and abiding passion, the Navy, were hard to bear for a young man who was only 34 years old at the outset of more than four years' idleness.

He therefore kept in touch with the Admiralty and tried to catch the eye of the authorities in hopes of winning a command. Part of this strategy was to bring 'interest' to bear, and just as in 1842 Cresswell had entered the Navy originally through the good offices of his cousin, the Northumberland MP, Baker Cresswell, now he tried the influence of his neighbouring MP, Charles Buxton. At least, Admiralty officials were obliged to reply to MP's letters:

November 11th, 1862

My dear Mr Buxton

Captain Cresswell's character quite justifies the interest you take in him, and the Duke of Somerset* is quite aware of his wish and of his fitness for employment and I have no doubt he will have every fair consideration as opportunities for employment present themselves, but it is one of the necessary evils of the service that officers on promotion remain so long unemployed. I was four years myself and when I got my first ship was even then the junior Captain employed.

Yours very truly,

John Moore.†

C. Buxton Esq. M.P.

Nothing came of this immediately, but Cresswell's campaign for employment continued:

Friday February 13th, 1863

Dearest Mother

I saw the Duke of Somerset yesterday. He was for him wonderfully civil, and although he gave me every reason to hope for early employment, he did not define any thing or any ship. He pointed me to a chair and let me talk and he let me talk until I did not know what more to say.

I told him how highly Sir J Packington‡ and Sir M Seymour had recognised my services, I claimed being the first person that ever went round America, I pointed out Lecky's case to him, and explained it. He did not seem to know any reason for his being employed except the Peiho forts, the same thing I was promoted for.

I spoke of my pirate affair after I was promoted to a Captain and told him that if he would fairly view my services he must see that I was entitled to employment.

I went to dine last night with the celebrated Joe Litton, Ossie was with us, and a lot of his Regt.

---

* Edward Adolphus, 12th Duke of Somerset, KG, First Lord of the Admiralty 1859–1866, member of the Adminstrations of Lord Palmerston and Lord John Russell.
† Captain John Moore, serving in the Admiralty in 1862.
‡ Sir John Packington, Bt., First Lord of the Admiralty, 1858.

He, Ossie, returned to Aldershot by a late train. We went after a 2 hours dinner to the Olympia and I got home a few minutes before 12. Uncle William and Uncle Oswald breakfasted at 21 this morning. I believe I shall be alone in my glory tonight at dinner.

I shall, if all goes well come by the London Colchester Ipswich line. Leave London 9.15, get to Norwich at 2.50.

I want to make some calls on Saturday afternoon and be home for hunting on Monday early.

I am going to call on Admiral Eden and Chas. Buxton this afternoon,
> Your very affect. Son,
> S. Gurney Creswell.

> Bank House, Lynn, Norfolk, March 30th, 1863

My dear Charles Buxton

Believing that you are so kind as to take a good deal of interest in my career in the Naval Service, I wish to tell you how I am now situated.

I went to the first Levee of the Duke of Somerset on Feb 12th. He was very civil to me. He had been tolerably civil last year, and had we had war with America over the *Trent* affair I believe I should have had a ship then.

I fancy your letter to Captain Moore had much to do with my gracious reception the other day, and although the Duke did not give me any thing definite he certainly held out the expectation of my being employed very soon.

I think it would have been well for me if Captain Moore had remained at the Admiralty as I know nothing of his successor.

At this juncture, when several ships are about to be commissioned a word from Sir F. Gray might do me infinite good if you see your the way to use a little influence with him. I cannot tell you how I weary for active employment on my own element, but I would not even for that ask anything of you or of anyone not fitting for them to do.

Pray give my kind regards to Mrs Buxton & Believe me
> Yours very faithfully,
> S. Gurney Cresswell.

The weary waiting was to continue for nearly another six months, until the long-awaited letter came.

Admiralty, September 5th, 1863

My dear Sir

I am desired by the Duke of Somerset to offer you the Command of the *Scylla*, now at Sheerness, to be Commissioned next week for service in China. Will you be so good as to let me have your answer on Monday morning?

        Very faithfully yours.

            Robert Hall.

Captain Cresswell, RN.

For reasons which will emerge, this letter was not to provide the gratification of ambition fulfilled, but was the prelude to the short, and very painful shattering of Cresswell's hopes and plans. It is not without irony that one of the principal actors in these dramatic events was the same Captain Robert Hall whose conduct on the staff of Lord Elgin and Admiral Seymour in China had so irritated Cresswell when commander of HMS *Surprise* in 1858.

But before the blow fell which was to end his hopes less than a fortnight later, Cresswell experienced some of the effects of his appointment, like this letter pleading 'interest' on behalf of another would-be sailor.

Upper Surrey Street, Norwich, Sept 11th, 1863

Dear Cresswell

Addison* called on me this morning to inform me of your having *at last* got a ship, and I congratulate you very much upon it as I hear it is a *good* one worth waiting for.

I write just to remind you of your promise about the nomination for my son. His name is Walter Lloyd Bignold, and he was 13 on the 15th July last.

I am sure you must be very busy just now, but when you can spare five minutes I shall be glad to hear from you on the subject.

        Yrs very faithfully,

            Edward Bignold.

---

* Brother to Cresswell.

Whether more or less welcome was this letter from Cresswell's former commander in HMS *Investigator*, Captain Sir Robert M'Clure, which neatly hits off M'Clure's character combining friendship with an irrepressible streak of school-masterliness.

United Service Club, London, Sept 11th, 1863

My dear Cresswell

I have just seen yr. appt. to *Scylla* with much pleasure. I am sure you will let me say a few words to you.

The Service has much altered since we were last employed, therefore study the Instructions and always have them to fall back upon if ever you have to justify your conduct, particularly with regard to Discipline, Punishment and Black List.

Don't let the authority out of your own hands, delegate a sufficient amount to yr. 1st Lt. to uphold Discipline and not to be always referring to you in small matters. Recollect that you must always be the Big Joss, always have the Defaulters before you at the morning Quarters, which ought to be the Parade of the Day when all offences should be brought before you and (except in cases of Mutiny) only receive complaints at that time. It will save many upsets as officers will have time for reflection. And you yourself upon such subjects take the night to sleep over it, your judgement will generally then be correct.

Be courteous but not too intimate with yr. officers, support your 1st Lt. if you have confidence in him, if not you had better part. Be careful of the Officers Messes, and to the Mids., impress upon them to avoid bad company and not get into debt. This will generally keep them straight.

There is now generally too lax a discipline, commence as you intend to go on, keep the reins *tight* with steady hand, and mind don't gall by capricious orders and conducts. This is a general view that guides myself, & I send them to you with every good wish for yr. success.

Believe me
Yrs very sincerely
Robt. M'Clure

But it was not to be. Cresswell was unable to take up the long-cherished appointment, since his health had collapsed in the matter of hours between his receiving his letter of Appointment, and his joining the ship at Sheerness.

By wretched chance when Captain Hall wrote the letter of appointment, on Saturday, September 5th, Cresswell was staying with his cousins at Cresswell in Northumberland. Instead of being sent to Cresswell's London agent, it was sent to King's Lynn, and did not reach Cresswell in the north until *after* Monday the 7th, the day on which Captain Hall sought a reply. The letter did not reach him in Northumberland until Wednesday, September 9th.

In spite of his best efforts, Cresswell did not arrive in Sheerness until Thursday the 10th, after a nerve-wracking journey during which he was in dread of losing the command because of his lateness.

The strain of the journey and his apprehension actually made Cresswell ill, with a severe bilious attack accompanied by nervous prostration. It was evident that he could not take up his command, as the *Scylla* was due to leave for China within a matter of weeks.

The officer responsible for the Sheerness squadron was Vice Admiral Sir George Lambert, and on September 17th, a week after Cresswell had arrived in Sheerness, wrote to the First Lord (The Duke of Somerset) to say that Cresswell was unfit to serve. Captain Hall replied to Sir George the next day:

Private   Admiralty, Sept 18th, 1863

My dear Sir George

I have read your letter of yesterday to the Duke of Somerset, and am desired by His Grace to say that it is evident that Capt Cresswell is not in a fit state of mind to take the *Scylla* to sea.

The Duke is desirous of sparing Captain Cresswell's feelings as much as possible, and would therefore wish that the application to be relieved from the Command should come from himself. His Grace, therefore, directs me to request that you will be so good as to Communicate with Mrs Cresswell and suggest to her that it would be well to urge her son to request to be superceded on the score of his health.

I am writing a note to Mrs Cresswell also by this post, to prepare her for your Communication.

Very faithfully yours

Robert Hall.

Vice Admiral Sir George Lambert, KCB.

P.S. As I do not know Mrs Cresswell's address may I trouble you to have the enclosed forwarded.

Private   Admiralty, Sept 18th, 1863

Dear Madam

From Communications which have reached the Admiralty, the Duke of Somerset fears that the state of your son's health is not equal to the arduous duties he would have to fulfil as Captain of the *Scylla*. The Duke is aware of the good and gallant services which Captain Cresswell has performed, having indeed selected him for a Command on account of them, and therefore desires to make his temporary retirement from active Service as easy to him as possible.

I am consequently desired by His Grace to suggest to you, that it is very desirable that you should induce your son to apply to be relieved from the Command of the *Scylla*, on the ground of ill health, and the destination of the ship. I am also to express the Duke's regret that it is necessary to make this Communication to you, but from the information he possesses it is out of his power to adopt any other course.

I am, dear Madam,

Very faithfully yours

Robert Hall.

This letter was forwarded by Sir George Lambert to Rachel Cresswell, and it is likely that he took the opportunity to include with it a short note in his own hand suggesting the terms in which Rachel Cresswell should write to the First Lord. The note, which remained in Rachel Cresswell's correspondence, would have given the minimum information needed about Cresswell's health, and would have stressed the temporary nature of his indisposition. The suggested wording was:

The very short interval that must elapse before the *Scylla* is reported ready for sea will not allow sufficient time for my Son to recover from his present temporary illness. I therefore trust when his health is restored your Grace will appoint him to another Command to make up for this great disappointment.

Instead, Rachel Cresswell wrote to the First Lord a letter which can only have been damaging to Cresswell's chances of ever sailing in the Navy again. It is the letter of a caring and protective mother, not the dry, but safer, formula suggested by Sir George:

Fountain Hotel, Sheerness, Sept 19th

My Lord Duke

A very painful duty devolves upon me as the Mother of Captain Gurney Cresswell. Since his return from China nearly five years ago, my son has from time to time after unusual fatigue and excitement suffered from short but severe bilious attacks accompanied with considerable nervousness, but always passing entirely away.

When I joined him here on Friday the 11th I found him ill. He had become so the day after his arrival in London after an arduous night's journey from Northumberland where some days *after date* he had received Captain Hall's letter with your Grace's offer of the command of the *Scylla*.

My son is so very much better that I should pronounce him all but well were it not that Sir George Lambert differs from me in this opinion. My son considers that under these circumstances he is bound in honour and duty to the Service to relinquish the command of the *Scylla* if your Grace will be able to accept it the time being so short before the *Scylla* will be ready for sea.

The Arctic climate for so many years, with almost starvation for eighteen months, China twice, once for more than five years, constant occupation between times and for two years after his last return home, being my faithful companion in nursing his father through a most painful illness originating from the long and terrible suspense of our son's absence in the *Investigator* have shaken his health.*

---

* Francis Cresswell died in March, 1861, two years' after his son's return home in 1859.

Unreasonable it may have been, but his constant wearing desire for Employment has also told upon him. Never was man more devoted to his Profession, and his services and standing have as I believe not been below the average.

He places himself entirely in the hands of your Grace, but if he is to live, if he is to recover from this most bitter disappointment it must be from the belief that, having done that which he considers his duty now he will again be employed should it please God to restore his health so as to entirely, as to satisfy your Grace of his fitness for it.

> I am, My Lord Duke,
> Yours obediently,
> Rachel E Cresswell.

Rachel Cresswell's detailed account of the stress suffered by her son is likely to have had the opposite effect, in the Admiralty, to what she hoped as a devoted mother. She also sent a similar latter to Robert Hall, on the same day.

To: Capt. Robert Hall, Admiralty.

The Fountain Hotel, Sheerness, Sept 19th, 1863

Dear Sir

It would be difficult for me to thank you sufficiently for the kind courtesy of feeling of your letter, or too warmly to express my appreciation of the Duke of Somerset's consideration for my son and myself.

Captain Gurney Cresswell has always had his address at his agents.

It was unfortunate that your letter offering him the Command of the *Scylla* was in consequence of being addressed to Lynn, and a Sunday intervening, five days before it reached him.

This delay distressed my son exceedingly, fearing it might lose him the ship, your having requested an answer on Monday morning (the 7th); and the night journey after a hard day's shooting with this dread upon his mind I believe to have been one cause of the severe attack of liver, and upon his nerves which followed it.

I had written to the Duke of Somerset before your letter reached me, may I ask you to explain this to his Grace and entreat for me his forgiveness for not writing another letter in its place as the substance of all I wished to say is there. Will you be good enough to tell his Grace with my warmest thanks that the hope held out to my son of future Employment should restored health be given him will I believe do more with the blessing of God to ensure his full recovery than any other human means could effect. I must Ever remember with Gratitude Sir George Lambert's kindness and sympathy during these miserably anxious days.

There is one thing that would immensely spare my son when his retirement is mentioned under the head of 'Naval Intelligence' that it may be clearly stated that the cause is 'illness'. I believe your own kind feelings will have already suggested this to you but you will forgive my mentioning it. The same post will bring for you a letter from my son as he considers it his duty to communicate with yourself directly.

> Believe me dear Sir
> > Yours sincerely & very gratefully,
> > Rachel E Cresswell.

There remained nothing to be done, but for Samuel Gurney Cresswell to write, formally asking to be relieved of command of the *Scylla*, to Admiral Lambert, and to receive his reply:

> To Vice-Admiral Sir Geo Lambert, September 19th, 1863

Dear Sir

On fully considering the events of the last few days, together with the doubts entertained by yourself & others of my health standing the climate of China, I have come to the conclusion that my duty to the Service to which I have the honour to belong requires me to request that I may be relieved from the command of the *Scylla*. I beg in conclusion to thank you most heartily for your kindess to me since I have been here, and I am deeply sensible of the consideration evinced toward me by the Duke of Somerset. I trust and fully believe that in a few months my health will be so thoroughly restored that His Grace may think well to Employ me again.

I shall of course do all in my power towards getting the *Scylla* ready for sea until my successor is appointed.

> (Yours etc.)
> > Captain Gurney Cresswell.

Admiralty House, Sheerness, September 20th, 1863

My dear Captain Cresswell

In reply to your letter I think you have acted quite right and I can only hope and trust the decision you have come to may turn out in every way to your future welfare both as regards your health and prospects in your profession.

As regards myself I can assure you that it has been a most painful duty I have had to perform, but I felt I had no other course to pursue than to follow what I thought due to the Service and yourself.

Believe me yours
very faithfully
George Lambert.

Cresswell's naval life was at an end, in spite of the efforts of his fellow officers appointed to the *Scylla*, who had wanted him to accept the command. It seems likely that he was already in poor health before the crisis of September, 1863 since his mother's journal records a visit to Eastbourne, earlier that summer saying he was 'unwell'.

Clearly the new disappointment took its toll, on top of the strains of previous years. He was obliged to return to Lynn and the Bank House, which still stands beside the river Ouse, overlooking the shipping passing to and from the port, and from which he set out with such high hopes and naïve excitement twenty-one years earlier.

Two glimpses of Cresswell in enforced retirement remain. He enjoyed playing whist with neighbours and relations in Lynn, but according to one observer, 'he must win . . .' so his attention was diverted by one player, while another arranged the cards under pretence of shuffling the pack 'so that the Captain had all the honours'.

And in 1865 he achieved a long ambition to see installed at St Margaret's church in the town a rose window above the altar at the east end in memory of his father, Francis Cresswell, and in Thanksgiving for his delivery from the Arctic a dozen years earlier.

But he was clearly now very ill, and as his mother records her return home after a visit away to stay with another ailing son, Ossie:

'He was overjoyed to see me. Never can I forget his look of intense pleasure. We spent six quiet loving days together, he quite himself, though unable to speak, his face full of response and expression. Then came a few hours of strife and trial, and he was gone – August 14th, 1867', six weeks short of his fortieth birthday.

Index